LAWYERS
AND THE
LAW

THE DREYFUS FAMILY MONEY MANAGEMENT SERVICE

How to Think of
LAWYERS
AND THE LAW

By MARTIN MAYER

and the Editors of Dreyfus Publications

illustrated by Richard Erdoes

DREYFUS PUBLICATIONS LTD. NEW YORK

MARTIN MAYER has long been a student of the interaction of citizens and the law and lawyers. Among his many books are: *The Lawyers, The Schools, New Breed on Wall Street, About Television, Madison Avenue, U.S.A.* A versatile writer of wide-ranging interests, he is also the regular writer of the department on recordings for *Esquire*.

THE DREYFUS FAMILY MONEY MANAGEMENT SERVICE

Jay Gold
VICE-PRESIDENT, EDITORIAL

Spero Yianilos
ASSISTANT EDITOR

Jane Smollar
EDITORIAL ASSISTANT

DREYFUS PUBLICATIONS LTD.

Jerome S. Hardy
PRESIDENT

Heinz E. Eller
EXECUTIVE VICE-PRESIDENT

Daniel Maclean
LEGAL DEPARTMENT

Sally J. Reich
VICE-PRESIDENT

Robert F. Dubuss
FINANCIAL ADVISOR

William Flaherty
Patrick Rooney
BUSINESS OFFICE

Linda G. Glovitz
OPERATIONS COORDINATOR

Marilyn C. Case
ADMINISTRATIVE ASSISTANT

CONTENTS

6

A NOTE TO THE READER

This book, like its companion volumes in this series, has been planned to be as functional as it is informative. For that reason, the typographic design for the text specifies exceptionally wide margins. These are meant to be used for anything that will be helpful to you: for notetaking, reminders to yourself or even doing arithmetical calculations. The editors hope you will find the margins useful.

The stock for these books was selected in part because it can be written on equally well with pencil, or ballpoint or felt-tipped pen.

The colored rules you will find scattered throughout the book are used to emphasize salient portions of the text.

— THE EDITORS

CHAPTER I

"Pay the Two Dollars"

Lawyers are not often good news. Their "open and aboveboard profession," as the Western writer Gene Rhodes once put it, is "living off the unlucky." Usually they tell you either that you shouldn't have done something or that you can't do something. The difference between a dictatorship and a free society, after all, is that in a dictatorship the law and lawyers tell you what's permitted, while in a democracy they tell you only what's forbidden. Whenever anyone living in a democracy writes about a utopia, he leaves lawyers out of it, because if everybody behaved himself all the time there wouldn't be any need for lawyers, and not much need for law.

But the man or woman who never has occasion for contact with a lawyer probably is not very lucky,

Unlike the situation in a totalitarian society, where
the law says what's permitted, democratic law
simply tells what is not permitted.

either. It means he has never inherited anything of
any substance, because only a lawyer can oversee the
distribution of an estate. It means he never bought a
piece of property, because lawyers are necessary to
draw up the contract of sale, the "deed" that conveys
ownership of permanent property such as land. And
it means his own assets are too small to make it sensible for him to prepare a will.

Lawyers are needed when you're in a fight, when
you're trying to make a deal, when you have to be
absolutely sure where you stand, and when you're
thinking of doing something that might cause you
trouble.

Lawyers' functions, in short, are fighting, negotiating, securing and counseling.

Obviously, it's useful to have someone around who
can serve such functions, and one of the great lux-
uries of the really rich is that they have lawyers on
call to help them. But it *is* a luxury, because a lawyer's
help doesn't come cheap. And even when you can
afford it, you may sometimes be better off accepting
what the world has brought you — taking your lumps,
or making the best deal you can get on your own —
rather than involving yourself with the complications
of legal process.

One of the classic stories of the old vaudeville stage,

When you have a legal fight on your hands
— don't fight. Get a lawyer to do that for you,
because that is one of a number of situations
in which you cannot do without a lawyer.

good for five minutes in the hands of a talented come-
dian, was of the man who got a ticket for running a red
light and was furious with the police and the System
because, he said, the light hadn't changed until he
was halfway across.

Because he really wanted to beat the ticket, he
hired a lawyer, who coached him in a story about how
the light was busted and the cop had solicited a bribe.
He forgot some of the coaching, and under cross-
examination he lost his way in the story, and the judge
got mad and indicted him for perjury.

Court, jail, then the chair

During the course of his trial for perjury, he got so
mad at the judge he was cited for contempt of court
and put in jail for the night. His wife refused to believe
that story and walked out on him, and the next day
when he came to court he took a swing at his lawyer,
who stumbled backwards, hit his head on a metal
pipe and died of a skull fracture — for which, after
further vicissitudes, the man was duly electrocuted.

Murder.

The story was punctuated with a litany of advice
from a wise friend, to "pay the two dollars." That became the title of a funny book by a clerk of court in
New York, full of tales of the awful things that happen
to defendants and plaintiffs, witnesses and even lawyers, in a courtroom. But it's not entirely a joke: "Pay
the two dollars" is a reasonable rule of life.

One of the most useful books any businessman can
read is Robert Coulson's *How To Stay out of Court,*
which is about negotiating techniques and the uses

Because he refused to pay a $2 fine he thought was unfair, a righteous man — in the old vaudeville gag — started a chain of events that led him to the chair while his wiser friend kept saying: "Pay the $2."

of arbitration. (Coulson is executive vice-president and general counsel of the American Arbitration Association.) In a speech to his fellow lawyers in New York, Judge Learned Hand once said that "as a litigant I should dread a lawsuit beyond almost anything else short of sickness and death."

Legal philosophers have always regarded law as primarily a system for resolving disputes. Hiring lawyers, obviously, is an expensive way to do that, much more expensive than sitting down and working it out yourself.

A lawyer has to pay for a secretary, office space, telephone, law books and files and other supplies: $15,000 a year at the least. (The American Bar Association estimates the average solo lawyer's annual costs at $20,000, but that includes a $5,000 item to amortize the cost of the lawyer's education.) His only source of income is his fees for his time, and even if he is very busy and efficient he cannot expect to bill for more than about 1,500 hours a year. (The ABA estimates 1,320; most state bar associations say 1,200.)

After he has paid for what is often an expensive education, a lawyer needs a bundle just to set himself up in his profession with the necessary office space, books, staff, etc. And after that, of course, he needs money to keep going.

He needs $10 an hour at least to pay his office bills, before he can start feeding his children. If he is to bill for 1,500 hours a year and have an income of $22,500 before taxes, which is about the average for a lawyer these days, he must charge you at least $25 an hour for the time required by your case. Most state bar "minimum fee schedules" do call for $25 or $30 an hour. That includes time looking up the law, time holding your hand, time interviewing any witnesses you must have, time drawing up petitions and pleadings; then time in courtrooms comes on top of that, if necessary, at higher prices. Fees can get up into the thousands of dollars very quickly.

The first question that anyone thinking of hiring a lawyer must ask himself is whether the matter at hand is really worth spending a lot of money to resolve.

The impossibility of giving little things the full treatment was recognized early in this century with the organization of "small-claims courts," which serve storekeepers who haven't been paid and customers who got their jacket back from the dry cleaner with a hole in it; the man whose son was bitten by the neighbor's dog; the owner of the car dented at the supermarket by the careless driver of a bakery truck. Such matters do not deserve the attention of a lawyer, but they are a nagging nuisance to the people involved.

You can pick up the necessary form for a small-claims court action at any courthouse, and there's no need at all to hire a lawyer. If your opponent turns up with a lawyer, the judge (who might be a moonlighting young lawyer himself) will see to it that you're not at a disadvantage.

Time — hours spent working on a case for a client — is usually the determinant of a lawyer's fees. That, and the amount that he considers his time worth per hour. This is the time-honored method of figuring fees in most legal matters.

When you buy a house, however, you want a lawyer to make sure all the documents relating to the purchase are in first-class order, because a house is an extremely important purchase. But when you buy a refrigerator, even "on time" and after signing a contract almost as complicated as the contract for a house, you don't trouble to call in the lawyers.

Much the same sort of thinking goes into the decision to use or dispense with lawyers in a business deal: your office manager has authority to buy half a dozen typewriters on his own, but before he can lease an IBM 370 for $150,000 a year, you'll want your lawyer to look over the contract.

When the decisions come easily

Sometimes the decision is very easy: if you're charged with a crime, or want a divorce, or wish to change your will, you need a lawyer, whether he's

A few more instances in which you are usually better off having a lawyer represent you: when "the law" seeks to imprison you; when you're hospitalized as the result of an accident, when you're headed for a divorce.

expensive or cheap. If you hear that an Internal Revenue Service agent is coming to audit your tax return, you might not want a lawyer, because the presence of a lawyer might make the agent suspicious at just the time when you want to make him trusting.

Sometimes the decision is very difficult: if you've been in an accident and an insurance company's claims adjuster comes to see you, you may or may not be better off making a deal with him direct rather than starting a lawsuit. If you're in business and a customer sues, you may be better off calling him and trying to settle the matter between the two of you — maintaining the business connection into the future — than defending the case in court, which will cost you not only lawyer's fees but also, in all likelihood, any chance of selling to this customer ever again.

If possible, you should always have a cool head when you go to see a lawyer: that's part of the wisdom of "Pay the two dollars." Your personal outrage is not by itself a good enough reason to make other people take the time and expense required by a lawsuit.

The unfairness of making you pay a traffic ticket you didn't deserve really is less than the unfairness of making lawyers and a judge and court attendants and (if you're lucky) witnesses devote their time to your petty concern. Life would be intolerable, Lord

Justice Pollock once observed, if everybody demanded all his rights. Anyway, think of all the times when you should have got a ticket and didn't. As a purely practical matter, a cool head minimizes the costs of getting involved with the law.

Hotheadedness is a distinct disadvantage in dealing with legal matters. What heats you up might turn other people off.

As we go on in these pages, we shall look at what lawyers are likely to cost for different purposes, and try to measure whether the benefits they bring you are worth the cost — in money and in your time — that will inevitably be exacted. As our society gets more complicated, and richer, more and more people find themselves in situations where they do — or should — have dealings with lawyers. You can't escape lawyers by reading books about law, or even by becoming a lawyer yourself — one of the oldest gags in the profession says that a lawyer who represents himself in a case has a fool for a client. To take legal advice from someone who isn't a lawyer (or from a book) is the mark of an even worse fool. But you *can* make your own decisions about when you need a lawyer, and how to go about finding one, and what his services should cost.

In this book, we shall look both at situations where people unquestionably need lawyers and at situations where it might make sense for you to handle your problems yourself, even though they have a legal component.

Let's start with the occasion when a lawyer's help is indispensable — when you're in a fight, and you need someone to do your fighting for you.

CHAPTER II

Jim B.'s Scrape with the Law

Not long ago, a college junior named Jim B., who had never been in trouble much with anybody, let alone with the law, accepted an invitation from his roommate to go to a party off-campus, in Chicago, at a friend's apartment. The afternoon of the party, the roommate came down with the flu, and asked Jim to take over a box of supplies, which included some phonograph records, a case of beer and — unknown to Jim — some marijuana. The party was not especially wild or uninhibited. Everybody had his or her clothes on and was sitting or standing in the living room while the stereo blared. At a few minutes after one in the morning, a knock on the door proved to be not fellow partygoers but police, summoned by neighbors who found the records too noisy.

Unfortunately, about half the people at the party, including Jim, were smoking joints when the door opened, and the police smelled what was in the air. A sergeant asked the graduate student who rented the apartment where the rest of the stuff was, and he pointed to the box Jim had brought, which was standing on a table by the phonograph. The police searched the box, and found about eight ounces of marijuana still in a pipe-tobacco can in the box. The next question was, who brought the box; and presently Jim found himself in a precinct house in conversation with a detective.

Playing the important card

Before asking him a question, the detective gave Jim what the police call "a Miranda card," named for the Supreme Court decision that gives everyone the right to have his lawyer present in the room when the authorities question him. By now it was after two in the morning. Jim didn't know any lawyers. He had an uncle he could call in Chicago who could have recommended a lawyer, but that would have meant Jim's father would hear the next morning (if not that night) about the party and the marijuana and the arrest — and Jim didn't want that at all. He agreed to answer questions without anyone representing him in the room, and he signed a document waiving his right to counsel. Then he just told the truth, which included the fact that the marijuana had been in the box when it was opened. He hadn't known it was there beforehand, but there it was when he got to the party and opened the box.

Jim walked out of the police station about an hour later, troubled but not really very scared. It wasn't until three days later, when he was summoned to a grand jury room, that he found out how bad it was. His roommate, who had been interrogated at the college infirmary with a lawyer in attendance, had denied putting marijuana in the box, and a couple of those at the party had told the police that Jim didn't seem surprised when he opened the box and took out the can of "pipe tobacco." Jim was indicted for a felony, as a marijuana dealer; and now he made an emergency call to his father in Pittsburgh to get him a lawyer who could get him out of this.

> A lawyer to be with Jim at the police station the night of the arrest could have cost anywhere from $50 (for a habituee of the night courts) to $250 (for a man who had to climb out of bed in the middle of the night to do the job).

Criminal lawyers often hire young associates to make their "house calls": if the mission is to tell the client to shut up, no great amount of experience or talent is required.

Another $300 or so might have been necessary to pay a lawyer to confer with the district attorney on Jim's case the day after the arrest, to talk him out of a felony charge and find out what evidence there was, if any, to prove that the marijuana had come to the party in that box rather than in somebody's rain-coat pocket, and to lay the groundwork for a plea to a minor charge and a suspended sentence.

By the time Jim's father was alerted and a lawyer was consulted, Jim was in serious danger of a long jail sentence, and the lawyer's fee was going to bear some relationship to ability to pay. In this case, in fact, because Jim's father was a successful doctor, the lawyer charged $3,500.

> Like most fees in criminal cases, the money had to be paid in advance: criminal lawyers have learned through experience that it's hard to collect from a client after he's got off, and almost impossible to collect from him if he *hasn't* got off.

Fortunately, what the district attorney wanted in this case was a lead to the man who had supplied the marijuana, and he wanted to hold the threat of a felony conviction over Jim's head to make him talk. Jim's new lawyer convinced the D.A. that Jim really had told the truth at the station house — that the man who might know where the marijuana had been bought was the roommate, against whom the state did not have enough evidence even to bring a charge. Once the stories of the raid had faded from the newspapers, the district attorney reduced the charges against Jim to possession, and because it was his first offense Jim was allowed to plead guilty to an offense so minor that he got not only a suspended sentence but the right to petition to have the conviction taken

The booking officer at the station house is required to be
suspicious of anyone brought in to be booked. That's his job.

off his record if he stayed out of trouble for the next year. Still, it had been touch-and-go for a while, and very expensive for Jim's father.

The first moral of this story is that anyone picked up by the police on suspicion of a crime should grab for every legal right he can find, and should immediately hire a lawyer to help him find all of them.

This is not to argue that people who commit crimes should escape punishment: it's always better for society, and often better even for the guilty party, that people who break the rules should pay something for what they break. Indeed, one of the reasons people often fail to get a lawyer immediately when they are arrested is their own feeling that they ought to be punished, which produces a desire to cooperate with the police, up to and including confession.

But the police and the district attorney, by the nature of their business, are going to try to make whatever you did seem as serious a crime as they can fit to the facts. From their point of view it's much easier to reduce a charge later than it is to make the charge more serious; and a law enforcer can't be too careful. Besides, a few years as a cop or a D.A. will give any man a low and suspicious view of mankind.

In fact, though, things may not be so serious as you think they are. In Jim's case, it's possible that the police didn't have the right to search the box that contained the marijuana; and the prosecuting attorney can't use against you any evidence the police acquired illegally. Sometimes what you did isn't a crime at all: in the course of winning a fight, you may have beaten someone so badly he had to go to the hospital, but if he started it you're probably in the clear. Or you may have hit a pedestrian with your car, even killed him; you feel horribly guilty, but an accident isn't a crime.

Once you start talking, however, especially when you feel guilty, you may give the police reason to believe that you did commit a crime. A lawyer on the spot can protect you from that.

A policeman's lot is to suspect more than a touch of the devil in people who seem to be quite innocent members of society.

The second moral is that lawyers are always available.

Under the Supreme Court rules laid down in *Miranda*, the police are obliged to give you a lawyer's name and a telephone number to call if you don't know a lawyer yourself.

Remember that you don't have to keep the lawyer who helps you at the station house, and unless it's somebody you already know you shouldn't make any agreement with him that covers his services beyond this particular interrogation. Any lawyer is

Before a suspect is interrogated, he is by law entitled to be
given a card telling him of his rights, the so-called Miranda card,
and the opportunity to telephone for legal assistance.

competent to advise you about which questions you
should and which you should not answer when the
police have you in the back room, because if there's
the slightest doubt he will tell you not to answer. The
lawyer's services in that room are mostly psychological.

It's much easier for you to decline to answer what
might be a dangerous question if your reason for
refusal is your lawyer's advice. When you're alone
in the room with the police, you can't help feeling
that a refusal to answer makes it look as though you
have something to hide, or you don't have a good
explanation for what you did.

The third moral is that lawyers are in business, too. If you're broke, a court will find one for you at no cost to yourself.

Since *Miranda*, the legal aid societies and public defender offices have staffed up to provide counsel for people in the hands of the police. And despite a lot of mythology to the contrary, these lawyers for poor defendants are often at least as capable as the run-of-the-mine criminal lawyer, and at least as dedicated to serving their clients' interests. But, of course, they don't have much time; and because they are idealists, they tend to be most interested in the defendant who insists that he is (and actually may be) innocent. That may leave the normal defendant, who has done something to get himself in the pickle he's in, with the feeling that these charity lawyers don't really care.

What crime costs in legal costs

Anyway, people who can afford a lawyer are not supposed to take a free ride on the legal aid society (though in most states they can use the public defender's office, if they wish). And a private lawyer in a criminal matter is likely to charge you whatever he thinks you can pay: most of the bar association fee schedules do not include fees for criminal cases, probably because lawyers who work in this area quickly learn to take care of themselves.

(One association that does is Kentucky's, which sets a minimum of $1,000 for defending someone charged with a crime that carries life imprisonment as a possible penalty, $500 in a case where the penalties can run 5 to 25 years, down to $150 for a misdemeanor carrying a maximum sentence of less than 30 days.)

Anything beyond a barebones defense will cost a client more than any standard minimum, and a specialist in criminal law is likely to be full of ideas for developing defenses (new witnesses to find, prosecution witnesses to check up on), and all things of this sort will cost a defendant money. It's like the surgeon who sets his fee to match the patient's wallet, and can do so simply because the quality of the

In criminal matters, the lawyer's fee is apt to be tailored to his client's wallet rather than to the amount of time spent on a case.

work done by a surgeon, (or by a criminal lawyer) may be so desperately important to the patient or client.

Does "famous" equal "best"?

People who get caught in a mesh of criminal circumstance usually feel that they want the "best" lawyer available. They think wistfully of the famous names they have seen in the newspapers. This may be a mistake, because the talent necessary to get one's name in the newspapers does not necessarily relate closely to the talent necessary to get a client out of trouble.

For a quarter of a century, the best criminal lawyer in New York, by universal agreement, was the late Harris B. Steinberg, a quiet man who managed to handle a number of well-publicized cases (including, for example, the Mickey Jelke white-slavery case, in the headlines for months) without becoming at all well known to the general public. He did not try to get the last possible dollar out of his clients, either.

Every city has its equivalent of Harris Steinberg, and the leaders of the bar will know who he is, even though they don't do criminal work themselves.

Your best source of information about a lawyer to defend you against a criminal charge, then, is the lawyer who represents you in other matters.

Most people in cities, however, don't have a regular lawyer. Their best bet is to try to activate a grapevine, alerting some member of the family or some good friend who knows a successful lawyer, to solicit advice. If that fails, the best tactic is to go through the files of the local newspaper, looking not for the courtroom warrior but for the quiet man who represented any scions of the rich recently in trouble in this town. (You won't find him quoted, because he won't talk to the press, but his name will be in the story.)

If your case does not appear to be one that will require a great deal of time — if you're willing to plead guilty to something because you did something, and you want someone to negotiate a minimum penalty for you rather than go through the immensely time-consuming business of a trial — you may be able to afford one of the best criminal lawyers in town. Try to approach him through someone he knows rather than just walking in the front door, because he is probably choosy about the cases he takes; but if worst comes to worst simply make a phone call, cold: lawyers usually will listen to stories.

The one thing *not* to do is rely on the advice of the police sergeant or the bail bondsman, who may be picking up a little graft on the side by recommending lawyers to people who have been arrested.

Haled into the presence of impartial Justice, an accused,
whether innocent or guilty, needs help from someone
who knows how the lady's mind works — a lawyer.

For the first hours after an arrest, however, it's better to take the lawyer who is around the station house
than to do without representation at all. Tell him, in
the presence of witnesses, that you are engaging him
only for the representation during an interrogation:
you don't know what you may wish to do about representation later, if it turns out that there is a later.
You can't be sure how skilled a lawyer you need until
you know how much trouble you're in.

Let's look at the case of Jim B. in this focus, changing the story to illustrate the differences in how much legal help he might require.

Assume first that he is totally innocent. The marijuana did not arrive at the party in his box, but was stashed there for convenience by somebody else. He himself was smoking a Camel in his clean-cut way, not a reefer. He had never touched a cannabis plant in his life.

Under these circumstances, Jim would need a really first-class lawyer, well known to the prosecuting attorneys as an honest man, who could convey his certainty that Jim was clean and persuade them to drop the case. The circumstantial evidence — the marijuana in the box he brought and the denial by the roommate that *he* had put it there — would make the facts exceedingly dangerous before a jury.

Most people who get off completely after being arrested do so not because they or a brilliant lawyer convince a jury of their innocence, but because they persuade the police or the D.A. that they are clean or that the case against them is insufficient.

More than 60% of all arrests do not result in any formal action beyond arraignment. Jim, innocent, in other words, has more need of first-class representation than Jim guilty, which is unfair — but the world is unfair.

Often it costs an innocent person accused of a crime more
to prove that he is not guilty than it does for someone who is guilty.

Assume now the facts as stated originally, with
Jim as an unwitting courier and then a consumer at
the party. Almost any lawyer, contacted at once and
present at the interrogation in the station house,
could save him from the dangers that threatened him
once he had talked to the police.

He *was* guilty of possession, which might not
seem a crime to him but did to the law, and the lawyer's basic function would be to keep him from
incriminating himself beyond that point. In the
absence of his admission that the marijuana was in
the box when he opened it, the prosecution would
have had almost no chance to prove this key element

in any charge beyond mere possession. And given Jim's clean record, a judge in Illinois would almost certainly be lenient with him even without a recommendation for leniency by the prosecutor.

Once he had in effect accused himself of a felony, however, Jim needed a skilled practitioner to find a way out for him.

Assume, finally, that Jim had indeed procured the marijuana himself, and had supplied it to the party for a price, making up the story about the roommate. He would be well advised to hire a lawyer who has a reputation for warmth and understanding rather than for technical skill. The chances will be that despite his apparently clean record Jim has indulged himself in this direction before, and the prosecutor will have information from police agents that will lead him to want to prosecute Jim.

A lawyer to persuade him

Under these circumstances, Jim had better be prepared to cooperate with the law, and identify his source of supply, and more than anything else he needs a lawyer who can persuade *him* to forget childish codes of honor and blow the whistle on the larger criminal. In return for such assistance, the D.A. may very well be prepared to reduce the charge to

possession and arrange for a suspended sentence —
or even to grant immunity.

None of this is Perry Mason, of course; but Perry
Mason isn't part of the real world. Helping you handle criminal law troubles, a lawyer cannot be just a
fighter, because if he loses, you lose, and in a much
more damaging way. (The line heard around the
criminal courts is, "The lawyer always goes home.")

If you are unlucky enough to be charged with a
crime, you will need the legal skills of the negotiator
and the counselor more than those of the fighter. But
nothing a lawyer can do for you when you are in the
criminal-justice system will help much unless he is
also believable as a fighter. The prosecuting attorney
compromises and makes a deal mostly because he
doesn't have the time or the manpower to try all the
cases the police bring him. The leverage your lawyer

Clients of a criminal lawyer may find
themselves behind bars after a consultation,
but the lawyer, as the saying has it,
always goes home.

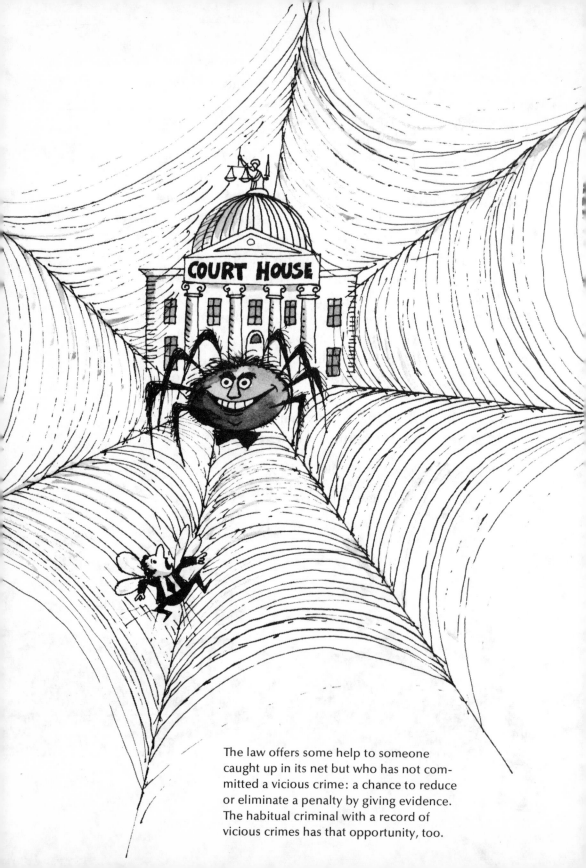

The law offers some help to someone caught up in its net but who has not committed a vicious crime: a chance to reduce or eliminate a penalty by giving evidence. The habitual criminal with a record of vicious crimes has that opportunity, too.

gives you results mostly from the implied threat that if the D.A. doesn't make a decent deal he will have to try the case.

Unfortunately, the same leverage is available to (and heavily used by) the drug peddler, the con man who victimizes the poor, the sadist who grinds broken pop bottles in his victims' faces. If you are one of those, you need a lawyer, too; and you will get one; but if his attitude includes elements of to-hell-with you, that's fair enough.

The plea bargaining that makes possible a degree of charity for people who are caught in the web of the law though they have not committed a vicious crime also serves the interests of the antisocial and dangerous. The lawyer serves them, too. He must; indeed, he should: the worst man in the world is entitled to representation before the law. But when a lawyer's victory sends a mugger back to the streets to mug again, he doesn't admire his triumph much more than you do. As Justice Holmes remarked, neither the judges nor the lawyers are in the court-room to "do justice"; they are there to play the game according to the rules.

To spend most of their professional lives with the scum of the earth is not an ennobling experience for most criminal lawyers. In other specialties of the bar, lawyers can usually convince themselves that in handling their clients' causes they are really fighting for the good, the true and the beautiful, or at least for fairness.

As has been pointed out by a great jurist, Oliver Wendell Holmes, lawyers and judges are not in court to render justice: they are there to win, abiding by the rules of the game, and hoping that justice will somehow be done at the same time.

The criminal bar tends to be much more cynical. The public rarely believes, as it is supposed to believe, that a man charged with a crime is innocent (until proven guilty); criminal lawyers almost never believe it.

Most criminal lawyers do not try very hard to make a client feel at ease. It's not uncommon for them to furnish their offices in a way that guarantees that when lawyer and client are both sitting down, the relative height of the chairs behind and beside the desk will leave the lawyer looking down on his client.

Nevertheless, criminal law is a real specialty of the bar, and even a rather arrogant and nasty-minded criminal lawyer will do better for you than a more sympathetic personality whose normal practice is in a less unhappy area of the law.

When you are charged with a crime, you simply have no choice as to whether you have a lawyer or not: you need one. The vast majority of those who try to talk themselves out of a criminal charge without the help of a lawyer — whether they are guilty or not — dig themselves in deeper. The criminal lawyer's fees will likely be high, and criminal lawyers who don't get paid will subtly or blatantly abandon their clients. But if you have been charged with a felony you are hiring a lawyer to save you literally years of your life, and it's hard to put a price on that.

A criminal lawyer — that's the fellow on the right here — often goes out of his way to make a client feel small in his presence.

CHAPTER III

"Divorces Can Be Made Only in Courtrooms"

Less than ten years ago, the head of a big New York corporation decided he had to be rid of his wife in some non-violent way, but she refused to give him a divorce. He shopped the city until he found a lawyer who told him that he could arrange a Mexican divorce that would take care of his problem.

He paid the lawyer a fee in six figures to set up an elaborate charade in Mexico, by which some very eminent people participated in assurances to a court that a local lawyer who said he represented the lady really had her authorization to perform that function.

By the time the game was complete, back in the United States half a dozen years later, the corporate executive, who had remarried, was paying a large fine for bigamy, the wife he had tried to trick was rolling in his dough, and the lawyer was disbarred. A man who really goes after it can get very bad advice.

Divorces, like criminal prosecutions, can seldom be accomplished without lawyers. Marriages may or may not be made in heaven: divorces can be made only in courtrooms. For divorces, as for criminal defenses, people with no money at all can now have their legal work done free: getting divorces has been by far the most frequent activity of the poverty-program law offices set up during the Johnson Administration.

In divorce work, as in criminal work, clients need lawyers who are convincing as fighters but especially talented as negotiators.

There the resemblance stops. People who have been accused of crimes need lawyers immediately; people who are contemplating divorce should try to work out their troubles as completely as possible by themselves or with the help of professional counselors before they put their fates in the hands of lawyers.

Under the Constitution, nearly all law that relates to family matters is left to the state governments, and each state has its own divorce law. But a marriage contracted in one state can be dissolved in another: the states give each other's laws and courts "full faith and credit." For years, couples in states with very restrictive divorce laws (like New York) used to arrange for divorces in states that had very permissive divorce laws. (Nevada and Idaho were the favorites, not because their laws were the easiest but because a visitor could acquire citizenship in the state, and thus the right to use the divorce courts, after only six weeks of residence.)

The validity of divorces granted in foreign countries, however, has always been a matter of some dispute. Where states do not formally accept the jurisdiction of the foreign court, divorces obtained there are worthless in the eyes of American law.

By the fall of 1973, divorce laws were greatly relaxed in nearly all states. In at least nine (California, Colorado, Florida, Hawaii, Iowa, Kentucky, Michigan, Nebraska and Washington) it was not even necessary to "prove" that one of the parties was "at fault" in the destruction of the marriage.

And nearly all the other states now permit divorce for any of a long string of reasons. (Some will require a substantial cooling-off period, though, before a divorce becomes "final.") But there is a hitch: divorce is easy, in any state, only when both parties really consent to it.

From the lawyer's point of view — and from the point of view of the client who has to pay the lawyer — there are two very different kinds of divorce: "uncontested" and "contested." According to the American Bar Association's summary of suggested minimum fees, the price of a lawyer's services in an uncontested divorce ranges all the way from $100 (in Broward County, Florida) to $1,000 (in Sacramento County, California). A husband has to figure on double that amount, because he will be paying his wife's lawyer as well as his own.

It would be nice, when it comes to dividing up household effects in a divorce settlement, to be able to do it simply: the way old-time stage magicians used to saw up a lady in a box.

Divorces are adversary proceedings in theory
even when they are amicable in fact, and the
law requires that each party have his or her
own lawyer. And custom dictates that the
husband pay for both.

Most states, and most counties, suggest a minimum fee of $250 or $300 to each lawyer for the simplest divorce, where husband and wife not only have agreed to end their marriage, but have also agreed on how much the husband will continue to contribute to the household he is leaving, and on the fair division of the money and house and furniture, the pets and the children, the two of them used to share.

Obviously, if these arrangements can be worked out by the parties themselves, their lawyers will have an easy job. It still isn't nothing: there are applications to be made to the court in proper form, and contracts to be drawn to make the deal enforceable, and statements to be prepared on both sides for presentation when the day comes. It's unlikely that the husband and wife really thought of everything their divorce settlement should include — Who will be responsible for young Bill's piano lessons? What happens if the wife sells the house and keeps the money and then demands that her former husband pay rent on an apartment? But an experienced lawyer will be able to tell quickly whether the couple has in fact accounted for all its assets and liabilities in planning a settlement; standard ritual questions will take care of the information problem.

In all the states where a divorce can be granted only on a finding that one party or the other is "at fault," the process can operate efficiently only if one or the other agrees in advance to take the blame for the failure of the marriage. (This sort of "collusion" between parties who are supposed to be adversaries is illegal, so some lawyers make the arrangements

themselves and later tell their clients what to say in court.)

By far the most common grounds for divorce, in court, is "cruelty." The wife claims her husband hit her, a friendly neighbor testifies to hearing such complaints from the lady on a number of occasions, the husband on the witness stand admits it, and the judge grants the divorce. In some states, mental cruelty, which may mean no more than telling a wife that her mother is a pain in the neck, will be accepted as a reason for divorce. But if the party who is supposed to have been cruel denies it, and testifies that the stories are all made up, the preparation for trial and even the trial itself may be long, unpleasant and expensive.

Being parted by a divorce
is no sweet sorrow to by-
standers to the quarrel
who do not want to part.

Even in the states where a marriage can be
dissolved on petition by a guilty party — where
fault is no longer considered — an agreement
in advance will probably be required if very
large legal fees are to be avoided.

For the main concern of the court in hearing an
application for divorce is rarely the simple question
of whether or not to force these people to continue
calling themselves man and wife.

Where there are children, the first question the
judge considers is which of the parents should have

Before most US state divorce laws became liberalized,
"cruelty" — physical and/or mental — was frequently
cited as grounds, and alleged to have been exercised by
the husband, no matter what the truth was.

the greater influence in raising them: who should
have "custody," and what "visiting rights" should be
conferred on the spouse who does not get custody.
Normally, mothers bring up children and fathers
visit them, taking them away perhaps on weekends
and for parts of summer vacations. Where such
arrangements are satisfactory to both parents, the
lawyers and the judge will simply go along. But if
either wants some custody or visitation arrangement
out of the ordinary, and the other does not agree,
the court will have to hear why, complete with witnesses; and the lawyers will have to present a case,
preparing witnesses, making motions, perhaps even
writing briefs.

Then there are the big time-devourers, the problems of property settlement and of alimony: who gets
what out of the dissolving household, and how large
a piece of the husband's earnings the wife is entitled
to receive for herself, and how much for the children.

Law is mostly about money and property, and
divorce law is no exception. In recent years, the
bargaining positions in such disputes have changed
drastically, and judges today are likely to tell a woman
who can hold a job that she ought to get one rather
than just sponge off her former husband. But it's never
simple, and if husband and wife can't come to an
agreement ahead of time the question of alimony is
going to be a nuisance for the judge, a lengthy job for

If the parties cannot agree in advance on alimony and support
arrangements, the chances are that the wife's
lawyer can crank quite a bit of money out of the husband.

the lawyers, and a substantial chunk of legal bills for the husband.

Most of the best divorce lawyers don't much like divorce. When you talk with them, the first thing they want to tell you is how strongly they support the conciliation machinery that is part of most state divorce laws, and how proud they are of the occasions when they have persuaded clients to give their marriage another chance. But they have also, of course, seen any number of cases where husbands and wives have really grown to hate each other, and divorce was necessary for the mental health of all concerned, including the children. Even then, the lawyers' function requires a knack for conciliation, because of the necessity to bring the parties to the marriage to some sort of agreement on what should happen in the divorce proceedings, before the matter gets to court.

The lawyer with the pleasant personality

One of the classic situations in divorce is that of the man who sees that his marriage is dead and consults with his business lawyer to get the names of the best divorce lawyers. He is told that one man is extremely competent but well known as a son of a bitch, while another is equally able and has a pleasant personality. So he takes the lawyer with the pleasant personality, because he has enough personal problems on his plate already; his wife winds up with the son of a bitch, and he takes a terrible bath in the final settlement.

Many lawyers will say that a divorce is the quintessential adversary situation: a true "zero sum game," where anything one player wins, the other player loses.

Neither side can stop fighting until the judge signs the decree. Because the divorce normally marks the end of the relationship, neither party has anything to gain for the future by behaving well now. And because what has gone wrong is inevitably so personal to both parties, emotions of an almost intolerable pitch are easily generated.

What the negotiations usually come down to is a question of who wants the divorce most. Probably the most important piece of information a client can give a divorce lawyer is whether there is another woman (or man) in the life of the displeased husband (or wife). In a situation where the husband has a girl friend and has made her pregnant and she wants to keep the baby, the wife's lawyer has an immense advantage in the negotiations: his opponent is under the strongest pressure to make a deal, make it now.

On the other hand, if it's the wife who demands the divorce because she has just found out about the husband's other woman, and he really *doesn't* want to marry her and finds the state of being already married very useful in fending her off — well, the wife's lawyer will have a hard time getting any sort of settlement, or even agreement on procedural detail, from his antagonist.

Situation made to order for the wife's lawyer: he has discovered
that the husband has made his mistress pregnant,
and said mistress wants to have and keep the baby.

In most situations, the wife's lawyer does not set a
fee. He will submit his bills to the court, the judge (or
his clerk) will examine them and cut them down
somewhat, and then the husband will be told to pay.
But these bills, too, can be negotiated before the
matter actually reaches the courtroom. Before a man
allows his lawyer to handle that negotiation for him,
however, he had better get his own fee firmly established. A husband's lawyer who feels that his fee will
be the same as that won by the wife's lawyer suffers a

dangerous conflict of interest when negotiating about how much his opponent should be paid.

Lawyers' fees in divorce actions are influenced also by the amount of property involved: nobody takes a "minimum fee" for representing a millionaire or his wife. One of the things that can make divorce conferences a little nastier than other conferences is the tendency for the husband to talk poor-mouth to the lawyers as well as his wife, while the wife tries to convince both counsel that the so-and-so can really afford much more than he's offering. If these questions are left to be settled by the judge, the husband will have to reveal his entire financial condition; and if he's been hiding something he may well be in trouble with his own lawyer as well as with everyone else in the case.

By far the best way to save money in a divorce action is to make reasonable decisions on property settlements and alimony before the lawyers become too intimately involved — and to remember that your lawyer will charge you time rates for every telephone call he makes or accepts on your behalf, as well as for the time at meetings and in courtrooms.

Divorce lawyers, like criminal lawyers, are often cynical about their work: they see so many people do so much cheating. But many of them are sad, personally affected by the tragedies, so often unnecessary, that walk into their offices. Some of the best of them are like priests or ministers, excellent listeners and sources of gentle good advice.

(A number of the best divorce lawyers, by the way, are Catholic. Where the client is also Catholic, a Catholic lawyer will ordinarily require him to give the conciliation office at the Chancery an opportunity to work on the problem. But the Church does not prevent Catholic lawyers from handling divorce cases.)

In Hollywood the divorce specialists tend to be rakish, and the lawyers who specialize in representing wives (there are such) are often handsome. But they are more likely to be rather dignified, with a manner that makes people ashamed to start screaming in their presence — and they can also be rather awesome when fees are being discussed.

A lawyer does not have to be a specialist to do a good job in a divorce action, especially if the parties are prepared to come to a reasonable agreement on the sticky issues of child custody and property settlements.

When a lot of money is involved, it's wise to deal with a firm that includes a tax specialist who can make sure the government doesn't get any more out of the separated households than the law absolutely requires. If the only goal is to put an end to a relationship gone bad, however, any local law office can probably handle the divorce case perfectly well, and it's at such one-man and two-man offices that the minimum fee is most likely to be what you will pay.

If you can patch up your marriage after proceedings have been started, ask the lawyer you've been consulting to add up the time he's spent on the case and bill you for that: you're not committed to pay him the full fee, and if he says you are tell him to sue you for it. He won't.

In fairness to the divorce lawyers, most of them will be glad to hear you've decided to give your marriage another chance, and they will keep their bills as low as their office budget allows. As one of them says, "When you send a big bill to a reconciled marriage, you just start them fighting all over again. . . ."

You'd be surprised how many divorce lawyers would sooner find a way to mend a marriage rather than aid in splitting it.

CHAPTER IV

You,
Your Car,
Your Lawyer

A law firm in a Western city keeps a car on the city's streets every night, with a radio tuned to the police frequency. Whenever the police radio reports a major automobile accident, the law firm's car hustles to the scene and its driver tries to sign up a victim of the accident as a client for his employers. Lawyers who specialize in personal-injury law have long been known as "ambulance chasers," and many are the accidentally injured persons who have found a lawyer's card in their coats when checking out of the hospital.

Something more than one-quarter of the entire income of the American bar in the last twenty years has come from the legal consequences of automobile accidents. What has made the service so expensive is that claims for personal injury, like divorces, have required the courts to assess "fault" before

Personal injury lawyers often don't wait
for clients to come to them.

damages can be awarded. Divorce, however, is a quid
pro quo — you get something for what you give away.
Nobody has anything to gain by admitting fault in an
accident.

> While most personal-injury cases are settled
> rather than tried, a victim cannot hope to
> receive a decent settlement unless he is in a
> position to prove the other fellow was at
> fault. The lawyers therefore have to prepare
> their cases even in situations where everyone
> knows that there is going to be a deal rather
> than a trial.

These arrangements may now be on their way out.
In ten states, including the states of the eastern sea-
board that have the greatest concentration of lawyers — New York, Massachusetts, Connecticut and

New Jersey — the legislatures have already adopted some form of "no fault" laws that make it much easier for victims of accidents to collect for all but major injuries without the help of lawyers. Under a no-fault system, anyone who is willing to take a settlement adding up to his actual provable losses — repair bills, medical bills, time lost from work — can collect up to $3,000-$10,000 (depending on the law) whether he or the other guy is to blame for the accident. He can go to court only if his injuries add up to damages beyond the cut-off figure; if he does go to court, the old "fault-liability" rules continue to apply.

The justification for no-fault accident liability is a very simple one: the old fault-liability system costs too much.

Under no-fault insurance plans, neither party in an accident has reason to hate the other unless damage is done to more than the car.

Of every dollar the driving public put up to buy automobile insurance, only 45¢ was coming back to the victims of accidents; the rest was being eaten up by the system. In contrast, medical insurance systems — Blue Cross and the like — return more than 90% of the premium dollar to help pay medical costs.

As the use of social insurance spreads through the society, many lawsuits over automobile accidents really determine only whether the costs of treating a victim's injuries will be paid for by his medical insurance or by the other driver's automobile insurance. Paying lawyers thousands of dollars and clogging the courts to resolve such disputes really does seem rather stupid.

For and against no-fault

Still, most states continue to use a fault-liability system, and the state legislatures are full of lawyers who don't wish to make waves. In one state (Illinois) the lawyers after losing in the state legislature were able to block a no-fault law in the courts, arguing that it was unconstitutional because it deprived citizens of their right to sue.

In general, the lawyers raise two arguments against no-fault:

1. that the new laws permit people to collect only for their out-of-pocket expenses, medical treatment and time lost from work, while under the fault-liability system victims of accidents are able to collect for "pain and suffering," too;

2. that fault-liability makes drivers more careful,

because they know they can be sued if they are "neg-ligent."

The answers to these arguments are:

1) awards for "pain and suffering" in fact serve not to recompense the sufferer but to pay his lawyer's bill; 2) nobody really thinks about legal liabilities while driving an automobile.

The true argument against no-fault was given off-the-record by a former president of the American Bar Association when asked why he had refused to support a no-fault bill in his own state legislature: "I know the current system is all wrong," he said, "but they keep telling me that a third of the lawyers in my state will go bankrupt if it's changed."

Though the fault-liability system as it now operates in America is essentially indefensible and will eventually disappear, it will be with us for a while longer. In most states it will be the way all accidents are handled, and in nearly all states it will be the procedure for cases where a lot of money is involved.

The fault-liability system does have elements that recommend it to the victims of accidents. Its foundation stone is the "contingent fee," which means that the lawyer is paid only if his client wins. This automatically makes him a fiery advocate of his client's cause; and because his fee is stated as a percentage of what his client receives, he becomes a fierce negotiator, too.

Because awards for damages can be very high — recoveries in six figures happen fairly often — highly skilled lawyers are attracted to this sort of work. And because the other fellow's insurance company will be paying the fee, the victim does not have to be rich or even middle-class to afford the best lawyer in the business. All he needs is an accident that really did him harm (or killed someone on whom he is dependent), plus a driver on the other side who carries heavy insurance protection.

Moreover, although the outside world looks on the lawyers who specialize in this field as greedy ambulance chasers, the fact is that they are among the less cynical members of their profession. Like all lawyers (and most other professionals) they must tailor the use of their time according to the fees that can be earned by it, but in personal-injury law their fees are determined by the client's needs rather than by his income. This means that they rarely find their own interests in conflict with those of the people they have pledged themselves to help.

And while personal-injury lawyers take a large share of what their clients recover, they can demonstrate through a whole series of studies done by impartial authorities that people who retain a lawyer usually wind up with better net receipts, after paying the fees, than people who do their own negotiating.

Personal-injury lawyers tend to be liberal in their thinking, and to feel that they are defending poor victims of society against a heartless circumstance —

and against the maneuverings of the big insurance companies. And because most of their clients wind up grateful to them, they feel that they have (and earn) warm lawyer-client relationships. Indeed, most of the time, a person injured in an automobile accident will find his lawyer friendly, sympathetic, helpful and solicitous. He may look like a vulture to an outside observer — he may even *be* a vulture — but he won't seem to be a vulture to his client.

Most states now require drivers to carry insurance, and even in those that don't the great majority of people who drive cars are insured. At the scene of an

To some outsiders — and many insiders, like insurance companies — personal-injury lawyers are indistinguishable from vultures. But not to clients who have gained awards through their work.

accident, a driver is usually required to give to all those involved in the accident his name, his insurance company's name and address, and the number of his insurance policy. He must then notify the insurance company (and, usually, the state licensing authorities) that he has been involved in an accident, and report the names of the others who were involved.

In general, if what has happened is worse than a fender-bender — and always if anyone has been injured — both parties should wait at the scene until a policeman comes, and should take the names and addresses of all witnesses. If anybody was shaken up at all in the accident, even if it looks like nothing now, a doctor should be consulted. Internal injuries from accidents aren't necessarily obvious at the moment they happen. It's not a bad idea, if you think you're going to have a lawsuit, for you or against you, to take pictures of the wrecks right after the accident. You can do this yourself or call a photographer: there is usually a listing for "Photographers (Legal)" in the Yellow Pages.

In theory, people who have been injured or whose property has been damaged in an accident seek recovery for their losses by suing the other party, who must defend himself or pay up.

In fact, of course, no insured driver ever has to handle his own defense: one of the things he's insured against is legal expenses, and his insurance company will supply a lawyer. One of the reasons it's so important to notify your insurance company whenever you are in an accident is that such notification puts the company's legal department to work.

It is also important to notify your insurance agent, especially if you have other business with him (home insurance or life insurance). He will use his influence with the insurance company (which counts on his selling efforts) to secure a quick payment of a legitimate claim, minimizing the nuisance to you.

Where only property damage has been done in an accident — nobody hurt, a few hundred dollars in repairs to the car — there should be no need for the owner of the damaged vehicle to hire a lawyer. Take the car to a repair shop and get an estimate of the cost. If you carry collision insurance, you then turn over this information to your own company, and they pay the bill, less any deductible amount, unless its appraiser cries foul.

If you don't have collision insurance (and many people don't), you have to enter into an adversary situation. Inform both the other driver and his insurance company of the size of the damages; and give

If an accident appears to have created grounds for a lawsuit — the one shown here, for example — it's helpful to have a picture that shows what happened.

them a couple of days to react. To be really safe, it is often a good idea to take the car to two different repair shops and get two estimates: the insurance company is entitled to have the work done as inexpensively as the local market allows.

Beware the conniving repair shop

Any repair shop that offers to overcharge the insurance company and split the difference with you should be dismissed from your consideration immediately. That's a crime, and you could get in trouble; and any large insurance company is likely to have had dealings with this scoundrel before, which may make it harder for you to collect on your claim.

Should the insurance company decline to pay your repair estimate, you should probably see a lawyer. Two hundred seventy-five bar associations run

referral services, and this repair-bill situation is where they are most useful.

In the half-dozen largest cities and in a few smaller cities (Denver is considered particularly good), an effort is made to match the lawyer's experience to the client's problems. In most places, though, the referral services are simply lists of lawyers willing to see anonymous clients inexpensively. The bar associations do not sort them out by specialty, and certainly do not guarantee their expertise at handling your particular problem.

But any lawyer can advise you on a fender-bender, and the consultation fee in the referral service is very low — in 138 of the 169 referral services that reported numbers to an American Bar Association survey in 1973, the fee for an initial half-hour interview with a referred client was $10 or less.

If the amount you are claiming falls within the limits of the small-claims courts in your state, the lawyer can give you instruction on how to use that procedure on your own behalf. If you need more than that, he can write a letter for you on his stationery, and follow it up with a telephone call to the company; and if you have an honest claim resulting from an accident in which you were yourself clearly not the party at fault, the odds are that the letter and phone call will produce payment. The insurance company will not wish to undertake the costs of defending a suit for a few hundred dollars unless it is sure to win; and it has no way of knowing whether your threat to sue is real or not.

When a car is not merely transportation
but a member of the family, an aggrieved owner
might feel that he needs a personal-injury lawyer.

A reputation for paying claims honestly and promptly is an asset to an insurance company, especially in its relations with its agents, who are likely to get an angry telephone call from a customer who is subpoenaed to give testimony about an accident some months ago which he thought the insurance company was taking care of. If the insurance company doesn't think you're ready to sue, of course, none of these arguments applies. The lawyer's real function in small claims is to give the insurance company a belief that you're serious.

Sometimes a lawyer will suggest that a recalcitrant insurance company's reaction to your claim for property damage can be improved if it is accompanied by a claim for personal injury: you've been having mysterious headaches or backaches ever since that awful incident. The ethical (and criminal) problems raised by such a suggestion are not easy to resolve. You can claim from the insurance company only the amount of damage you have suffered: you can't add on the cost of the lawyer, and except in extraordinary circumstances the courts won't add it on for you.

If an insurance company by refusing to pay a legitimate claim has driven you to the expense of a lawyer, it is hard to see why you rather than the company should be the loser for it. The lawyer's suggestion that you increase the size of your claim becomes under these circumstances a proposal to shift the burden of his fee to the shoulders of those who should, in all fairness, be paying it. The problem is that once you start lying, there may be no place you can stop — and you want, of course, to avoid perjury.

Any suggestion from a lawyer that you should fake an injury to make money for both of you should be turned down immediately, before it tempts you.

Where the only claim is one for damages to the car, no lawyer is likely to be very enthusiastic about your case. Still, a lawyer who specializes in this field, and does business every day with a claims adjuster from the company that insured the other party in your accident, may be able to get you your money with a single phone call to a friend.

If all you want him to do is write a letter and make a telephone call — if the money involved isn't worth the time it would take *you* to give depositions and testify in a trial — you may be able to make your arrangements with a lawyer on a flat fee basis, $50 or $100 for his time. But if there is any prospect of the matter actually going to trial, the lawyer will demand a percentage of the award, if he agrees to take a small case at all.

In any case which involves personal injury, with a chance to claim long-term disability or substantial "pain and suffering" or disfigurement as well as out-of-pocket losses, a lawyer will insist on a contingent fee arrangement that gives him a piece of the action if you win. In an automobile case, the fee is normally 33 1/3%, though the percentage may be negotiable down in cases where the potential award is very large; and, conversely, the lawyer may try for 50% in cases where the potential award is $500 or less. (Some group

An award to a plaintiff in a personal-injury case has to be split with the lawyer, who usually gets one-third.

legal service plans sponsored by trade unions provide that the lawyers who get clients from the plan will not charge more than 25% on their contingent fee.)

This fee covers the preparation of the case and its trial in a court of original jurisdiction; if the insurance company appeals the verdict, and the lawyer has to research and write briefs and argue before an appellate court, his fee usually rises to 40% of the total you recover. No discount is given, however, if the case is settled before trial, as most cases are: the lawyer's 33 1/3% stays the same.

And after the fee come the expenses

Moreover, that's just the fee. The lawyer is also entitled to deduct from your receipts all his out-of-pocket expenses directly related to your case, any witness fees he may have paid out on your behalf, the costs of transcripts of depositions, etc. On the average, these costs eat up another 10%-15% of jury awards. (The percentages may be lower if the case is settled before trial, because the lawyer's costs are lower.)

In some jurisdictions, judges frown on lawyers advancing to their clients the costs of proceeding with a case. While the lawyer you hire is your lawyer, he is also supposed to be an officer of the court, and his advocacy of your cause is supposed to be constrained by his obedience to the letter and the spirit of the law — and lots of judges worry, not without reason, that the lawyer who has actually sunk his own money into his client's case will behave unscrupulously to make sure he wins. But a hard-and-fast requirement that the plaintiff in the case pay his lawyer's expenses himself would keep poor people from suing, frustrating the purpose of the contingent fee, and while judges frown they will rarely interfere.

The one thing that really is forbidden is cash payments by the lawyer to his client, to persuade him to persist in his lawsuit and turn down an offer from the insurance company which the lawyer considers inadequate. The possibilities of abuse are of course obvious in any situation where the lawyer "invests" considerable capital in a client's case. But the question is not necessarily simple, because the world is full of accident victims who need cash *now* and may settle a claim for much less than it is "worth" if there is nobody to support them through what may be years of delay before a case comes to trial.

There are few court systems in the US where personal-injury cases are tried as quickly as one year after the date of the accident. Two years is routine, and there are a number of cities where delays of five years and even more can be expected in as many as half the cases.

Most commentators believe that the insurance companies like the delay, because it puts pressure both on the injured parties (who must pay the bills) and on the lawyers (who do not receive their fees until the case is over) to accept what may be an inadequate

Personal injury suits take a long time to settle, sometimes so long
that an injured person might wonder what the settlement fee is for.

offer. The companies themselves, however, argue that in our inflationary era they lose more by the increase in the average award as time goes on than they can hope to gain by financial pressure on the claimants and their lawyers.

Whoever is right in this argument, the fact that you must expect delays means that you can safely take your time in deciding whether or not you need a lawyer to represent you and which lawyer you want. No final decision should be made for at least a month after the occurrence of any accident that may have produced serious physical injury. The decision to retain a lawyer is in a sense as final as the decision to accept an insurance company's offer of settlement: either can, if taken wrongly, diminish your ultimate compensation.

In the next chapter, we shall discuss the various factors you should keep in mind as you consider whether or not to retain a lawyer to handle a claim for personal injury in an automobile accident.

CHAPTER V

You, Personal Injury and Your Lawyer

The dangers of accepting the insurance company's first offer for a personal-injury claim are obvious. The extent of injury and physical or psychological impairment, loss of time from work, career disabilities — all these are still unknown in the first days after an accident. But a contract for settlement of a claim, unless tainted by demonstrable fraud, will bind anyone who signs it. If your injuries later prove to be more serious than you thought, you cannot reopen the case.

If you have suffered an injury bad enough to require hospitalization, you will probably receive a visit from an insurance company claims agent soon after you return home — sometimes even in the hospital, though this is regarded as bad form. Always say you are interested in arriving at a settlement, and take the agent's card — but not his first offer.

You need time. Don't worry about being late in paying the medical bills: hospitals are used to late payment and doctors, more often than not, can afford to wait.

A month or so after the end of your direct medical treatment for the consequences of the accident, you should know for sure how high your immediate costs are. It is good policy to make a list, detailing all the items of expense — medical care, help around the house, loss of wages, etc.

Whom should the law punish? Reward?

For bargaining purposes, it is perfectly proper to include in your costs medical and hospital bills that were in fact paid by Blue Cross or some other health insurer; you're not obliged to tell a claims agent, though you may be obliged later to tell a court, about your own medical insurance. And, incidentally, this isn't cheating: after all, why should someone who *doesn't* carry medical insurance collect more than someone who does in a claim for damages following an accident? That would punish the foresighted and reward the foolhardy, which is exactly what the law should not do.

At this point it might also make sense to consult a lawyer and see whether, for a small fee, he will give you some idea of what he considers the value of your claims. You will need a certain strength of character to tell a lawyer that you have a personal-injury claim that you wish to process yourself, and all you want from him, at least for the time being, is an estimate of how much you should bargain for. But a little strength of character will help you a great deal in your negotiations with the claims agent, too, and there's no harm getting some practice.

In general, insurance company claims agents are prepared to offer you something a little better than your documented out-of-pocket costs, to compensate you for the pain and annoyance you have had to suffer.

You ought not to take less than double what you can prove, and three times the out-of-pocket expenses is by no means an unusual settlement. Your threat in the negotiations, of course, is that you will retain a lawyer and bring suit, which will greatly increase the insurance company's costs with relation to this claim. It may be a good idea to set a deadline: "If we don't have a deal by two weeks from Friday, I'm going to get a lawyer and bring suit."

Don't accept a claims agent's statement that he isn't authorized to settle for more than a number he's quoting; he can always, after all, go back for a new authorization. But he probably will not be empowered to go much over three times your out-of-pocket expenses unless he has a strong feeling that a lawyer

A little threat to a claims adjuster in a personal injury dispute — I'll sue! — may get him to increase the settlement without costing you the one-third of the award that a lawyer would take.

may find a much better case for you than you know you have.

If you are making a specific claim for pain or future disability, you will have to submit to an examination by the insurance company's doctor. All authorities advise you to deal with this doctor as a man haled into the police station deals with the cops: give nothing more than the civilian equivalent of name, rank and serial number. Anything you say to a doctor can be, and probably will be, used against you in evidence if it becomes necessary for you to sue.

Hiring a lawyer to handle your claim is as final an action as accepting a settlement offer: once that contract with the lawyer is signed, you are stuck with it.

If you change your mind about the insurance company's offer the next day, your lawyer can (and will), without doing a lick of work, collect one-third of your settlement. And there's nothing you can do about it, because your contract has authorized the lawyer to collect on your behalf, and to deduct his fee (and his expenses) from the check before passing on what's left to you.

If you later get tired of this lawyer, or feel he isn't really doing a job for you, you may find it virtually impossible to get rid of him. There have been a number of cases of accident victims who hired a second lawyer to represent them without securing the consent and withdrawal of the first lawyer — and who then had to pay fees to both.

When a lawyer is too expensive

Going to a lawyer will cost you time and trouble, and in smaller cases it may cost you money. Many, perhaps most, people who sue for relatively minor injuries resulting from automobile accidents recover less than their out-of-pocket expenses. Remember, in order to pay the lawyer's fee and leave you even, the final settlement or jury award must be at least 50% more than what the company is offering. (A third off $3,000 leaves you exactly where you would be with all of $2,000 — the 33 1/3% fee is bigger than it looks, and the lawyer's expenses come on top of that.)

Unless there are some continuing disabilities or pain which persuade a jury that you should be compensated for future damages resulting from the accident, it's unlikely that even a very smart lawyer will be able to get more than 50% over an offer of double your out-of-pocket costs in connection with the accident.

All these problems are manageable if you can persuade your lawyer to sign a contract that gives him only a share of what you collect over and above an existing offer from the insurance company. If you switch lawyers in midstream you should insist that your new lawyer work on that basis, to avoid the situation where both lawyers try to take fees from your final award for settlement.

If you are crippled, or in continuing pain, or have suffered some disability that diminishes your future earnings potential (torn knee ligaments for an athlete, a scar for a model, a bum back for a secretary, a broken thumb for a rug dealer), you do need a lawyer, and he will earn his keep.

Lawyers are used to thinking in the multiplier terms that legitimately apply when you have suffered some disability that will — or even just may — remain with you for years, with unknown effects. In negotiation, they can ask for sums of money that would take the ordinary citizen's breath away. They can develop cases through examination of expert witnesses whose testimony will carry weight with juries. From sources of information not easily available to people outside their business they know the size of awards juries have in fact been giving to people who have suffered accidents and injuries similar to yours.

In the case of an accident with future implications, it is not uncommon for lawyers to win for their clients settlements or jury awards five and ten times as large as the best offer made by a claims agent early in the proceedings.

If a personal injury affects a claimant's efficacy in his or her work, damage awards can be higher. Examples: a basketball player whose knee has been hurt; a rug dealer with a busted thumb; a secretary with an aching back; a show girl with scars that show.

The only exception to the rule that you need a lawyer to handle claims growing out of more serious accidents is the instance in which the driver of the car that did the damage is a relatively poor man who carried only limited insurance. An offer of $8,000 from an insurance company that is not liable for more than $10,000 is much better than an offer of $40,000 from a company that might be forced to pay out a quarter of a million. If a claims agent tells you that his company's liability is limited because of a minimum policy, get it in writing.

There is of course always some risk that a personal-injury case will be lost by the defendant. In most states, in legal theory, a victim cannot recover in a lawsuit unless *all* the fault in the accident can be attributed to the other party. This stems from the so-called "contributory negligence" rule. In fact, however, juries refuse to apply this old rule and judges often fail to tell them that they should.

How to know that you'll win

In general, if you were involved in an accident in which the fault was *mostly* that of the other party, you are likely to win the case, whatever the insurance company claims agent may tell you. The contingent fee system gives you information here, too: if a lawyer is willing to work on a case for which he will not be paid unless he wins, he must believe you're going to collect.

If he's willing to work . . . that's the danger. The

lawyer is an independent professional man, who never knows what business will walk in his door tomorrow. It's hard for him to turn down a case even if he's really too busy to work at it; and it's not easy for him to continue giving the necessary attention to your case if something bigger comes to him tomorrow.

When you talk to a lawyer about the possibility of his handling your personal-injury suit, find out whether he expects to do the work himself or turn it over to a specialist.

You have nothing to lose by his "assigning" the case: you pay the same fee, and your influence with the specialist lawyer is likely to be greater if you have a friend from whom the specialist hopes to get other business in the future.

Your lawyer is paid a part of the fee at the end: this "fee splitting" is condemned by many experts in legal ethics, but it often happens. The specialist justifies it by giving the lawyer who sent him the case some small part of the job to do — usually, keeping you out of the specialist's hair.

If the lawyer to whom you are speaking says he will handle the case himself, ask him for his experience in the field, and whether he expects to prepare the case for trial, and how. A lawyer who plans on doing nothing but making some telephone calls to a claims agent at the insurance company is scarcely worth hiring for a case where the potential award is high. You won't be able to judge the quality of his thinking about your case, of course; but you should be able to get some sense of whether or not he knows what he is talking about.

How many cases are waiting?

Most personal-injury lawyers will tell you about very large awards won by previous clients, and that's fine. Ask also how many personal-injury cases he now has in his office, waiting for settlement or trial.

Not many lawyers can keep track of more than two dozen or so cases at once; if he has a hundred cases pending in his office, he should have at least three associates. If you have an enthusiastic recommendation from former clients, or from another lawyer who is a friend of yours, you might be willing to hire a firm which has as many as 50 cases per lawyer pending in the office, but you probably have to expect a longer wait before anything happens on your case — and less attention to your problems.

If possible, you want the lawyer to carry the costs of the case: telephone calls and taxi fares, filing fees, stenographic transcripts or depositions before trial, subpoena fees, payments to expert witnesses and the like. Some lawyers won't do it; most will.

Don't accept a flat first statement that the office never undertakes costs; if it would be inconvenient for you to invest money in your case, tell the lawyer your story, and tell him you will have to think about whether you can afford to do things his way. It may be in your interest to undertake these costs yourself: a lawyer who feels that carrying a case to trial involves a risk to him, because of the increasing investment he has to make in the costs, may be under pressure to settle too quickly and too cheaply. There is no implication here that the lawyer is dishonest, or not looking out for your interests. It's just that he's human, too.

Cases that are not settled in the first six months or so after the lawyer files suit are likely to wait until trial date, which may be some years off.

They move out of the claims agent's office at the insurance company and into the legal department, which may even mean an outside law firm. That office is also, and always, crowded and busy. Appointments for examinations before trial must be made for the convenience of both lawyers as well as the convenience of the witnesses. Court dockets are full, and your case must wait its turn.

Because the insurance company's lawyer is paid better for a case that actually goes to court than for a case he settles in the office, it is not uncommon for him to delay a settlement until the day the case is called on the court calendar — or even longer, if that day is inconvenient for him: courts always grant lawyers postponements for almost any reason.

Level with your lawyer from the beginning about

your ability to endure a long delay before receiving compensation for your injury. He can probably get you a better settlement if the goal from the beginning is to go about it fairly fast. He won't do as well if he starts out with no urgency but then suddenly has to start making urgent phone calls to the insurance company because by then you need the compensation.

One kind of case that should almost always be settled fairly quickly, even at some sacrifice of potential recovery, is the wrongful-death action, in which a widow is trying to secure compensation for what would have been her husband's earnings.

Until this century, it was rare for courts to allow recoveries in death cases: the claim was considered to have died with the injured party. (This rule still holds in libel cases, by the way: "you can't libel a dead man." Worse: if a man who has been libeled dies during the trial of his action, the case ends, because his heirs can't inherit the cause of action.)

In states where the rule against recovery in wrongful-death cases persisted into the age of the auto-

Suits for personal damage or wrongful death take so long to settle simply because there are so many of them.

It's perfectly safe to slander an innocent man — if he's dead. Or if you know he will die soon. His heirs cannot continue the action.

mobile, the black humor of the legal profession pretended that taxi companies instructed their drivers that if they hit a pedestrian they should be careful to back up and make sure they had killed him.

Now statutes do permit recoveries in wrongful-death cases, but they are narrowly written, and the amount of the recovery is cut and dried, a projection of the dead man's expected income, with the total reduced (maybe) by deduction of what he would have spent on himself and (if the insurance company's lawyer is good or lucky) by the interest that will be earned on any lump-sum award.

If there appears to be the slightest possibility that the widow will remarry, insurance companies will delay trial of cases of this sort as long as they can, because juries are reluctant to give really large awards for the death of the late husband when the plaintiff is being supported by a new husband.

In theory, the defense lawyer cannot mention the fact that the lady has remarried: nothing that has happened subsequent to the demise of the victim is legally relevant to a wrongful-death action.

In fact, the lawyer always finds a way to let the jury know.

"Black" joke in the legal profession: taxi company tells a driver who has hit a man, and hurt him, to back up and run over him again to make sure he's dead. Because before the automobile age, in wrongful-death cases the claim was presumed to die with the injured party.

CHAPTER VI

Workmen's Comp., Attractive Nuisances and Malpractice

Injuries from automobile accidents are unique because a complete system exists to enable you to collect compensation routinely, without help from a lawyer or from the courts.

By law accidents must be reported to the state department that supervises road safety, and by contract to insurance companies. Thus the insurance company is immediately put on notice that there may be a claim, and can act accordingly. If you are the potential plaintiff, you know the name and address of the person you might have to sue, and the name and address of the insurance company that will have to pay the judgment against him if you do sue and win. And you can start a process in motion with a simple letter.

The insurance company employs regiments of claims agents whose life's work is to settle cases before they come to court. The problem can be handled by people who have had no special training in — and no special information of — the law.

> Indeed, one reason why no-fault auto insurance legislation can be contemplated is that a system already exists to handle the great majority of automobile accident injury cases outside the framework of legal procedure.

Non-legal procedures may ultimately develop in the workmen's compensation field, too, because a federal Occupational Safety and Health Act, new in 1973, requires employers to report all accidents on the job. Heretofore, unfortunately, a large proportion of accidents have not been reported at all, and many injured workers have received much less than they should have, even under what were often inadequate Workmen's Compensation law payments. Unless the union or the employer himself helps start the proceedings (and the employer often won't help at all, because his insurance rates go up if he has too many accidents in his plant), an injured worker often doesn't know how to begin.

This is a pity because there is no legal problem whatever in collecting for an accident on the job: Workmen's Compensation was the original no-fault law. Victims can recover only for actual expenses

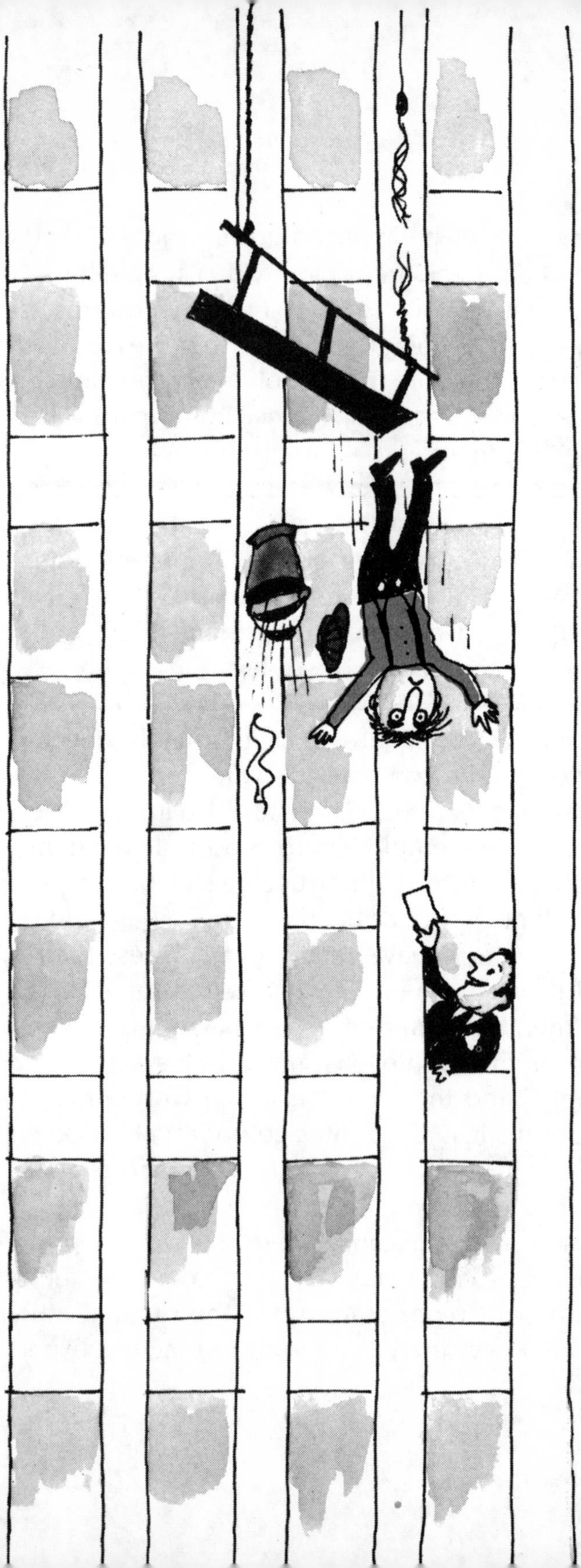

and economic losses, though these can be projected into the future.

Lawyers aren't very interested in workmen's compensation cases, except for those that fall under the federal Jones Act because the injury occurred on a ship. (The ship can be in harbor, even tied up to a dock; but the fact that the injury took place on a ship puts it under the special maritime — or "admiralty" — jurisdiction of the federal courts.)

In Jones Act cases, as in automobile accident cases, the lawyer can take a fee of one-third of the final award. In workmen's compensation cases, the state board awards the lawyer a fee which will consist of payment for the hours of time he can prove he really spent on the case. But the fee is not taken out of the money awarded to the injured person.

The best place to go for advice on getting compensation for an accident on the job is the union representing the workers in that shop. Most of the expertise necessary to make this sort of claim will be ready to hand at the union office, and whatever else is neces-

The personal-injury lawyer proffering his card to a falling window washer proffers in vain. For injuries sustained on the job, the man can swiftly get a Workmen's Compensation award through his union — without giving up a third to a lawyer.

sary can be arranged, at no cost to the employee, either through paraprofessionals trained to handle workmen's comp. cases or through the union's own lawyer. (Lawyers for seamen's and longshoremen's unions, which have a lot of Jones Act cases, build big firms on the economic foundation of such cases; other union law firms will have a couple of young lawyers expert in quick processing of "workmen's comp.")

If an employee doesn't have access to a union, the workmen's compensation case is another ideal situation in which to use the lawyer referral services of the local bar association. Most of the lawyers who

register with these services fall into two categories: men who want to do a little public service professionally, and men who can use a little more business. For the first group, workmen's comp. is clean work that does give human satisfactions; for the second, it pays adequately if not handsomely for time that might otherwise go unbilled.

The plumber's emphysema

Incidentally, there are also some workmen's comp. specialists who are especially valuable when there is a question as to whether or not the accident is work-

Same injury, sustained two different ways, brings two reactions from personal-injury lawyers. In the case of a man hurt on the job (right), a lawyer can receive as his fee only what Workmen's Compensation allows. Caused by an automobile, same damage might bring three times as much in settlement award, of which a lawyer can get one-third.

related. There was, for example, a recent case of a plumber in an eastern city who was incapacitated by emphysema. He thought it had something to do with all the buildings on which he had worked where there was asbestos in the air. An examiner turned him down because he smoked cigarettes: the lung infection might therefore be his own fault. The union found him an expert in workmen's compensation law. On

Man hurt by falling crate on dock is covered by Workmen's Compensation. Man hurt by falling crate aboard ship is covered by Jones Act, even if the ship at the moment is stationary at the dock. Man-on-ship would interest a personal-injury lawyer, for here he could get one-third of the award.

appeal the state board awarded him a lump-sum payment for lifetime disability.

> For most people the most important single reason to get a representative (or non-lawyer specialist) for a workmen's compensation claim is the fact that the lawyer gets the matter out of the context of their relations with the boss.

The *Chicago Daily News* recently carried the story of a man whose boss told him not to make any claim for an accident that had happened in the shop — the boss would take care of him; and now he owes $60,000 in medical bills, and the boss has fired him as accident-prone.

A claim for workmen's compensation is not a hostile act against an employer, and even the meanest-minded boss will understand that, even if he suffers an initial spasm of anger at being sued. Once the matter is in the hands of a lawyer, the injured worker and the boss never have to talk about it at all, which is the right way to handle these things.

A case against your old buddy

Another source of injury for which one can usually recover is a defective or improperly maintained piece of property — rickety staircase, uneven sidewalk, torn rug, defective chair. The chair can be in the house of a friend as well as in a restaurant. If you're visiting your old buddy Elmer and the cane bottom gives way and you wrench your back, you probably have a case.

It is not a friendly act to bring a case of this sort unless your friend is either very rich or has a home-owner's insurance policy. Even when he is insured you may find that suing him (and formally you must sue *him*, not the insurance company) will end your friendship. Nobody likes to be sued, even if the insurance company pays. But the costs of a slipped disc operation may hurt you more than the loss of the friendship.

These cases are complicated in form, with none of the automatic procedures that can be used in automobile accidents and workmen's compensation

A personal-injury lawsuit can be a very personal affair.
For example: if it begins when the injured party falls
through the bottom of a wornout chair in a friend's house.
If suit ensues, friend becomes former friend.

Someone who walks past signs clearly indicating danger,
and emerges shaken up by a severe electrical jolt,
has only weak grounds for a personal-injury suit.

cases. You will need a lawyer. As in the automobile cases, however, you don't have to worry about paying him; he'll take the case on a contingent fee.

Some "place-related" cases a lawyer may not take because he doesn't think you have a winner. Most accidents will yield recoveries only if you have some business being there.

If you walk through a door painted with a big skull and crossbones and the words DANGER: NO TRESPASSING, the law will not look kindly on your claim for damages because you received an electric shock that burned off the tip of your finger. You will also be out of luck if you didn't look where you were going — if you put your arm through a glass door because you were absorbed in an argument with somebody and making big gestures, it's your hard luck.

But people who invite other people to work in their factories or shop in their stores or catch the show in their theaters are obliged to make the premises safe, and will have to pay for any injuries resulting from a failure to exercise "due care." The same rules apply to people who invite other people to their homes for purely social purposes.

In some instances, there may be liability to complete strangers who are not invited at all. In general, a trespasser comes onto your property at his own risk, and if he gets hurt it's no concern of yours. But children are regarded as natural trespassers onto any property where there is an "attractive nuisance" — a swimming pool, perhaps, or a rock pile that invites climbers — and any injuries children sustain in such places may be grounds for a lawsuit.

You are also liable, incidentally — and this may be important in our up-tight time — for injuries suffered even by a trespasser if you have deliberately created the hazard. If you set a bear trap by the French door to catch a prowler who might come in from the garden, you can be sued for any injuries to his leg, and he can collect — even though he's in jail for breaking and entering.

Another kind of injury suit we owe to the persistence 60 years ago of a Scottish-American named Donald Macpherson. He took his new Buick out for a spin and found himself piled up on the side of the road: one of the wooden wheels had collapsed. He investigated, and found it had been made of wood that was rotting. He then sued for damages.

Today this seems a routine thing to do but in the 1910s it was rather preposterous. One of the best established doctrines in law was that a man could sue only someone with whom he had some immediate relationship. If you loaned a man your horse and he put it in a stable that burned down, you didn't sue the company that owned the stable, you sued the man;

It may seem unreasonable to you to be slapped with a personal-injury action from someone serving a jail sentence because he was convicted of trying to break and enter at your house. But if you set out a trap to catch him, and he got caught, and his leg got hurt, he might have grounds for a suit.

Macpherson v. Buick, way back in early years of the century, established the right of a purchaser to sue the manufacturer for selling him defective machinery or whatever.

he would have to pay you and then try to collect from the owners of the stable. If you bought a product that turned out to be no good, the only person you could sue would be the storekeeper.

This takes us back to fault liability. The storekeeper didn't owe you anything, because he hadn't done anything wrong: he'd just sold you what the manufacturer had sold him. In the end, then, nobody was legally liable for defective products. The person who was injured had no relationship with the manufacturer, who *was* at fault.

Macpherson's great victory

Judge Benjamin Cardozo, then of the New York State Court of Appeals (and later a Justice of the US Supreme Court) cut through all that nonsense with a single sharp opinion. At first, of course, what he wrote applied only to his own state of New York, but within ten years or so virtually all the other state high courts had copied *Macpherson v. Buick*.

Now "product liability" is part of the Uniform Commercial Code, which has been adopted in every state but Louisiana (where old French law still prevails).

If you suffer an injury as the result of a defective product, you can bring and win a lawsuit. And because you can win a lawsuit, you may be able to get a settlement without a suit.

For this sort of case, however — for the sweater advertised as nonflammable that caught fire when a cigarette ash dropped on it, the mislabeled medicine that made you sick, the television picture tube that exploded — you need a lawyer. Every part of the case is very tricky: proof of defect, proof of actual harm done you by the faulty product, proof of damages resulting from that harm. Moreover, the best

cases of this sort will be brought not by an individual acting solely on his own behalf but by a group of people all victimized by the product, and that group is put together by a lawyer.

Thus, a group of the death cases resulting from an airplane crash will be joined together, with one lawyer representing all the plaintiffs. Once liability has been established by the one case, all the others are fairly easily settled (though sometimes separate trials are necessary to permit juries to assess damages). The people whose vision was harmed by the drug Mer-29, the parents of the deformed thalidomide children in England and Germany, home-buyers whose sewers back up — these and others bring "class actions" on behalf of themselves and others similarly harmed. The end result may be individual settlements or a pot from which members of the group draw their share — after legal fees are deducted.

Such "class actions" are also available to you in situations where you have suffered losses by some-

In class-action suits, a number of plaintiffs, with the same plaint against an adversary party, sue on the same grounds and at the same time in the same suit. Often one lawyer, or one team of lawyers, represents the whole caboodle.

one's financial misbehavior — by an insider trading in a stock, for example. These are fault-liability situations of the purest hue, where fault may be hard to prove. If you made a bad investment, you have to take the consequences. The only time the law can be any help to you is when somebody deliberately did you in, and even then you would probably have to show that he broke the law in the process.

One of the injuries recently added to the list for which you can recover is the one resulting from a doctor's mistake. It is not easy to be entirely enthusiastic about this development in the law. Doctor's shouldn't make mistakes. When they do, it's sort of an Act of God — bad news. By convincing the courts that doctors are likely to be at fault when anything goes wrong in a medical procedure (*res ipsa loquitur*, they say — the thing speaks for itself), lawyers have made a big change in the way the world works. Positively, they have won some cash compensation for misery for many unlucky patients. Negatively, they have raised

the cost of practicing medicine substantially and they
have poisoned relations between doctors and society.

In New York and Los Angeles, the average doctor
now has to pay about $12,000 a year for "malprac-
tice" insurance.

Today, a doctor driving along the highway
will shoot right past the scene of an accident,
without stopping to offer his services — a
thing that would have been unthinkable 25
years ago. For the moment he stops to help,
he lays himself open to a lawsuit.

Some states have "Good Samaritan" laws which
excuse people from some legal liability for mistakes
when they voluntarily try to help others; but the
courts, fearing phony samaritans, have cut down
the scope and effectiveness of such laws.

Anyway, if something goes wrong today in connection with a hospital stay or a doctor's care, and you
sustain injuries that cost you money or unnecessary
pain, you may very well be able to collect from the
doctor's or the hospital's insurance company.

You will need a lawyer even to get started in such
a case. Because you have to prove the doctor is at
fault (and other doctors are likely to be reluctant to
give you much help against their colleague), you must
be guided by an expert in what constitutes proof. In
these cases, too, lawyers work on a contingent fee.
Again, they may or may not assume the costs of pro-

ceeding with the case, which in medical malpractice suits may be heavy, because the doctors who do testify on your side will have to be paid; negotiate it with the lawyer in advance.

Do make sure in your own mind that what happened to you was really your doctor's fault.

It's dirty pool to use the leverage of a malpractice suit to make a doctor cut his fee; if you think he has overcharged you, just don't pay as much as he asked, and explain why.

That's a matter for negotiation, not for blackmail. Remember, a suit for malpractice, unlike a suit against an employer for an accident, is a direct attack on a

Operation successful but a surgical instrument missing. Surgeon might later find malpractice suit brought against him if the missing instrument is found inside the patient.

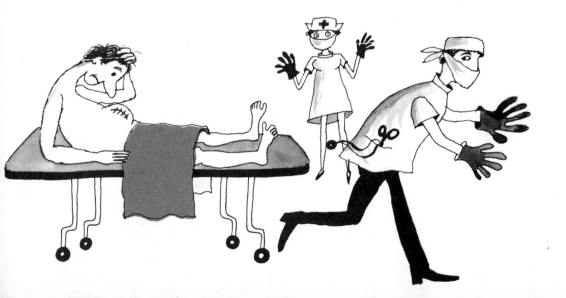

professional man's competence. At the least, it will boost his insurance premiums; at the worst, it diminishes his reputation, practice and income. Unless you feel your doctor should be punished for what he did, bringing a malpractice suit is a nasty thing to do.

Some lawyers may tell you that a malpractice suit is "nothing personal against your doctor, just business." Your doctor will take it personally, and he will be right. Still, if he left a scalpel in your gut when he sewed you up, he deserves to pay something for it, if only as a reminder to be more careful next time.

CHAPTER VII

The Biggest Deal of All: Land

We look now to the sad story of Bill J., who bought a country house atop a little cliff about 20 feet high, beside a lake in Minnesota. What really sold him the house was its seclusion, the chance for real privacy. The little beach on the lake could be reached only by stairs that began right behind his house, and there were woods on both sides that hid the presence of any other houses. There was a path that went into the woods on the right; the real estate broker said it had been there since Indian times.

It wasn't much of a house, but, on the other hand, it wasn't very expensive. Bill and his family saw it on a spring weekend, and everybody loved it; and before returning to St. Paul, he signed a binder, an informal contract to buy.

Bill took possession of the house in early June, and

The purchasers of this house — in wintertime — loved it for its seclusion and setting at lakeside. But a longtime, unwritten easement brought hordes of summer people to the steps in front of their house — legally.

he and his wife put it in shape lovingly, replacing a couple of the beds, painting the kitchen, preparing a flower garden. Then, on the July 4th weekend, processions began appearing on the path, men, women and children with bathing suits and towels, coming out of the woods and down the steps to Bill's beach and lake.

As politely as he could, he told the visitors that this was a private house and his land and his steps. The

strangers just shook their heads and said they'd been using this path and those stairs for years, it was the way to go swimming and used by everybody at the trailer camp on the other side of the woods.

The unwritten easement — but legal

Bill called the police, who refused to interfere. Then he called his lawyer, who said he'd look into the matter. A few days later the lawyer came by for a visit and gave Bill as bad a shock as he'd had in his whole life. That path had been in use, for years and years, by people who wanted to swim in the lake. One of the reasons Bill had been able to buy the house cheaper than he had expected was the fact that the public had an "easement" across the land — not written down anywhere, just customary, but legal enough for all that, because it had always been true, within the memory of the oldest inhabitants.

Experiences like Bill's, not uncommon, are the reason most people now recognize that they should never buy a house, summer or winter, without advice from a lawyer.

• Doctors find they can't have their office in the home they bought for combined use as residence and surgery: the zoning laws forbid.

• There are suburban townships where a recent municipal law requires all homeowners, within the next year, to stop using their cesspools and pay for a link from their plumbing to the town sewer main some miles away.

• A fellow who did some work on the roof, for which he hasn't been paid, may be about to slap a "mechanic's lien" on your new house, and that lien may become your indebtedness, though you never knew about it when you signed your contract to buy.

• There are horrendous stories, often true, of people who bought a house and paid for it, and then found some years later that their title to the land was faulty, and somebody else had a reasonable claim to the ownership of their home.

• Or there hadn't been any recent survey, and suddenly the new neighbor next door begins to build a driveway through what you had thought was *your* privet hedge. . . .

The list is endless; only lawyers know it all; only lawyers, with a few well-chosen clauses in the contracts, can protect you.

Land law is the root of American law. It could be argued that the real reason lawyers are so much more important in the US than they are in any other country is the fact that nobody knew who owned the land as the nation spread west.

There was no king to make awards and stand behind them; and only the law and the lawyers could really secure anyone's ownership of land.

Land is there forever: of all property, it is the most likely to be passed on by inheritance, which triggers yet another set of needs for certainty.

Everything that has to do with the ownership of land must be just so, in writing, in proper form, officially recorded, preserved at a public records office.

If what you are buying is a home, in most states you need the signatures of both husband and wife as sellers: a husband can't sell his wife's home away from her without her consent.

Lawyers in real estate matters are not fighters for you in the normal course of events: this isn't courtroom stuff, and there really isn't a full-fledged "adversary relationship" between buyer and seller. But the lawyers are indispensable advisors, and their function in securing you against future trouble is essential. By the standard of our first criterion for deciding whether or not you need a lawyer, moreover, real estate qualifies easily: it's important enough. There is no other purchase you can make where a few hundred dollars' extra cost to make sure you've got everything right can be justified so simply.

Unfortunately, the lawyers know all this, too, and the fees charged for work in connection with the purchase of a house are probably the best payment per hour the run-of-the-mill lawyer gets.

Indeed, it is a case connected with the buying of a house that is probably going to destroy the bar associations' minimum fee schedule arrangements, because the fee was high enough to provoke another lawyer.

In 1972, Lewis Goldfarb, who works as a government lawyer for the Federal Trade Commission in Washington, arranged to buy a house in Fairfax County, Virginia. His purchase price was $54,500. Before he could get a mortgage from a bank, he had to show clear title to the property. He went to a lawyer's office in Fairfax County to buy a title search of the kind required by Virginia law. The price quoted him was $522.50.

That struck him as too much money for too little work, so he went to another lawyer — where he was told, again, that the price was $522.50. In all, Gold-farb went to 19 lawyers in Fairfax County, and every one of them quoted a price of $522.50.

From "minimum fee" to "suggested value"

As an employee of the Federal Trade Commission, Goldfarb is well acquainted with the anti-trust laws. And if ever he saw the anti-trust laws being violated, it was here. He went to court to get an injunction against the Fairfax County lawyers to prohibit them from price fixing in restraint of trade, and he also demanded treble damages of $1.2 million for himself and others similarly situated. (Another "class action.") In January 1973, a federal judge ruled that the county fee schedule was indeed a violation of the anti-trust laws, and gave Goldfarb enough of what he asked for (damages are still being debated at this writing) to convince bar associations around the country that they had better shift from a "minimum fee" system to a "suggested value" system; and even that may go.

The fees Goldfarb was asked to pay ran about one percent of the price of the property for a title search alone. In those states where lawyers take responsibility for the validity of titles, that's about what they charge.

(In a number of states, this work is done by title insurance companies; their fee includes the cost of an insurance policy, which guarantees that you will never lose money because a cloud is cast on your title to the house and land.)

It's good pay for the rather limited amount of work involved, at least in counties where the courthouse records are in good shape. But it's a real bonanza in cities, where lawyers may get one percent of a $10-million deal just for searching the title — and if the building changes hands the next year may get another one percent of, say, $11 million, to do the work all over again.

Searching the title is only one part of the job a lawyer must be paid to do in connection with the purchase and sale of a house. He must analyze each contract and mortgage document you are asked to sign, to make sure your interests have been protected — no easements, no mechanic's liens, no unpaid taxes or assessments, exact descriptions of the property (including surveys), the details of the deed, zoning regulations, date of possession, terms of payment and of mortgage, and more.

You cannot rely on the seller's lawyer to secure your interests in any of these matters; and the lawyer for the bank that is writing the mortgage couldn't care less what sort of deal you have, so long as he can see to it that the bank is protected. You as mortgagor pay the fees of the bank's lawyer, and the cost of the bank's title search and title insurance — but you have to pay again to have your own lawyer do it all for you.

Supervising the purchase or sale of a house is in fact a lot of work for a lawyer, and to top it off he must also attend the "closing," where all the documents (and there are very likely half a dozen of them) will be signed, sealed, and delivered. But for what you are paying him, it would not be unreasonable for you to demand even more work than that; and the intelligent way to use a lawyer when buying a house is to bring him in from very early in the negotiations — certainly, before you sign anything.

One of the four central functions of lawyers is to negotiate, and buying a house is an activity where negotiating skills are crucial. Most people buying a house are bad negotiators: they have fallen in love with it, they see themselves living here, the cost is already more than they had planned to spend so a few bucks more doesn't seem like so much, they need a place to live, they want to get it over with.

After a day of looking at houses you're in no better condition to negotiate seriously for the one you liked best than you would be if you'd been pub-crawling all day. Shopping for houses addles the mind.

And the real estate broker who's been showing you around is not that much help. His main interest, quite openly, is in making a sale: he would rather see you happy than otherwise, but naturally that consideration cannot be uppermost in his mind. Legally, moreover, he is the seller's agent, not yours.

When you have found the house you want, you should call in your lawyer, or find a lawyer if you don't already have one, and let him handle your end of the negotiations from the earliest possible moment. If there are disputes about which are the fixtures the seller must leave and which are the furnishings he may cart away — or about which party is liable if fire or flood or tornado totals the house between the day the contract of sale is signed and the day of the closing — you want your lawyer, who understands all the implications, to uphold your end.

Most people do understand the importance of having a lawyer when buying a house: all across the country, legal referral services report real estate work the second-largest (after divorce) among the categories of calls for a lawyer's help.

You will, of course, have to pay a lawyer for the time he spends negotiating on your behalf, but it should be possible to get a credit for part of that fee when the time comes to pay the large fees associated with the conclusion of the deal.

How large these fees will be varies considerably from state to state. For a title search, in the states where lawyers do this work, the minimum fee (apart from

People shopping for a house often fall in love with one
that isn't really right for them. A lawyer consulted in time
can help homebuyers avoid costly and sad mistakes.

questions of price and percentage) ranged in 1970 from $100 in Illinois and $150 in Pennsylvania, all the way up to $500 in Florida. (These figures were median figures for the state as a whole; each county bar association had its own minimum.)

As a rule of thumb, you should probably expect to pay between two and three percent of the price of the house for all the legal services associated with closing the deal in proper form (including the legal fees you must pay to the bank's attorneys in connection with the mortgage). For that kind of money, you are entitled to advice and to help in the negotiations as well as to the routine services associated with the closing.

One reason it's a good idea to get a lawyer started working on your behalf as early as possible is that sometimes the best service he can perform for you is to talk you out of a deal you thought you wanted to make.

If you are selling a house, you probably don't need quite the same degree of care in getting the i's dotted and the t's crossed. When the transaction is over, after all, you will have cash that does not have to be protected from other claimants, and not a house for which title must be absolutely secure.

Your real estate broker, who keeps five or six percent of the sale price, has considerable incentive to bargain on your behalf for the best price he can get you. Nevertheless, it's a good idea to have a lawyer look over any legal document you are going to sign, well before you sign it — to make sure, for example, that you don't promise a title that is really better than the one you have. And if a prospective purchaser's lawyer comes over to chat while the deal is being negotiated, it's probably a good idea to call your own lawyer in on the meeting.

Is it really cut and dried?

All the strictures that apply to buying a house apply also to buying a condominium. In fact, the problems may be worse here, because there is so much less experience with the obligations incurred by the purchaser of a condominium, and because it all looks so cut and dried, with standard forms being signed by all the buyers.

We know from the 1930s what happens to cooperative apartment houses in a bad depression: they go bust, the stock becomes worthless, the property is taken over by a bank, and the purchaser loses everything he put into buying his apartment. Whether condominiums would fare better, nobody knows.

And of course, there may never be another depression like that of the 1930s. Still, the fact remains that all the jointly owned apartment houses can be no stronger than their weakest link: once a few of the apartments are no longer occupied, the burden of maintaining the building must be split among fewer and fewer residents. Varying degrees of protection against trouble are built into the bylaws of cooperative apartment corporations and condominium deeds, and it is important to have a lawyer read these documents and explain to you — several times, if necessary — what it is you are committing yourself to do if the national economy, or your own economic destiny, does not follow the course you expect.

It is also an excellent idea, though relatively few people do it, to have a lawyer read through any lease you sign to rent an apartment.

There is no one "standard form lease"; every model of lease has lots of forms. It is important, for example, to get a warranty in the lease that the premises are safe and habitable; in the absence of such a warranty, in many states, you may be held liable for continuing to pay rent on a place in which legally you can't live. The author of an American Bar Association pamphlet on availability of legal services noted that the first lease *he* ever signed, personally, required him "to waive any cause of action he might acquire by virtue of the infestation of the leased apartment by vermin." To say the least, you don't want such a clause in your

Carefully reading his lease in his bug-ridden apartment, a hasty lessee may find that in signing it he waived any rights against pest protection.

lease, no matter how tightly printed and "standard form" it appears to be.

A lease may or may not give the tenant the right to sublease. The question of the tenant's right to renew the lease at its end, and the terms of renewal, ought to be spelled out in the document, but frequently are not. In most states (though not in those with rent control laws) a lease that simply terminates on a certain day, with no provision for renewal, leaves you at the mercy of the landlord; he can evict you without any reason at all. And most standard form leases hold you liable for the rent for the entire term of the lease, even if you have to move to another city. As a minimum precaution, you should get a lease that permits you to cancel on a month's notice — paying, perhaps, an extra month's rent for the privilege, to give the landlord additional time to find a new tenant.

An experienced lawyer will know the provisions of the best "standard form lease" used in your locality, and will be able to show you in what ways your

Even if you are assured that the lease is "standard," have a lawyer read and interpret it for you.
There is no such "standard" lease.

lease is not as good for you as another one would be. Then you can decide, with his advice, how much you want to fight for. What you will get, of course, will be a function of your bargaining power: in a city or a suburb where the vacancy rate is 10%, you will be able to get a much better lease than you are likely to be offered in a city or suburb where the vacancy rate is one percent.

The cost of a consultation with a lawyer on the terms of the lease you have been offered will be trivial in view of the benefits you can receive from good advice. This is another area where the lawyer referral services of the local bar association will come in handy if you don't already have a family lawyer. The lawyer knows what it is you need to know; he doesn't have to research any law or take depositions from any witnesses or risk a day in court.

A small premium for happiness

A fee of $50 — $100, top — should do it; and to insure your happiness in an apartment for which you will be paying thousands of dollars in rents each year, that's a small premium to pay.

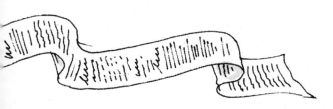

CHAPTER VIII

At the End, at the Beginning — and Some Stages In-Between

If you ask the man or woman on the street what it is a lawyer does that is most important for ordinary people, the answer is almost sure to come back: "He writes wills." Even the transfer of real estate is not so thoroughly policed by the law as the transfer of assets from someone who has just died to those still living who have some claim on it.

Wills do not take effect until they have been accepted by a court through a closely controlled process called "probate." What makes the problem so technical is the fact that the man (or woman) whose wishes are to be carried out can no longer tell those who must do so what he (or she) has in mind. With few exceptions, there must be a will in writing, and the writing must be specific. What is omitted from a will will probably not be done.

And if there is no will at all, the assets — the "estate" — of the deceased will be split up according to the state law governing "intestacy." These laws cut off from any distribution of assets all those not in direct family relationship, which means wife and children. (The parents of the deceased, for example, who may have been relying on him for their support, are entitled to nothing under intestacy laws; neither is a wife's child by a previous marriage, though the relationship may be as close as any in the family.)

Fuel for the political parties

The intestacy laws set up elaborate schemes for continuing supervision, by "guardians" appointed by probate court, of any assets allocated to children who have not reached the age of maturity. "Special guardianships" of this sort are the fuel that powers the political parties in the cities and states. They are one of the major reasons why politicians fight to preserve the custom of electing judges who after their election are beholden to the politicians, then the politicians are in a position to suggest who should be appointed as guardians and paid by fees allocated from the estate.

The expenses associated with this sort of guardianship tend to be high. No doubt, they were in the mind of a New Yorker who, dying a few years back, left all

Probate courts, and the rich fees that go with the guardianships that the (elected) probate judges can assign, finance local political party operations in many parts of the country.

his possessions to his lawyer and accountant on the grounds that they would wind up with everything anyway and it was cheaper to give it to them directly.

The lawyer's services in writing a will are now called "estate planning." When performed correctly they far transcend the business of setting words on paper. A will-writing session is next door to psychotherapy if the lawyer is performing his business properly.

He wants to know details of relationships with many people, the likelihood that today's marriage will produce tomorrow's divorce, the need (if any) to make provision for children as yet unborn, any friends to be taken care of that the "testator" would not like his widow to know about. (This last can be accomplished by leaving money to a third party whom you trust completely, with the instructions to pass it on.)

The lawyer has to know precisely how much the man preparing his will is worth, to make sure that he does not will people more than he has, which will result in scaling down all legacies proportionately, both the important bequests and the ones he included only because he thought he had so much money in his estate that he could be a sport. And, of course, there may be "tax consequences" — income tax, federal estate tax, state inheritance tax, etc. — which can be minimized in a well-drawn will or greatly increased in a poorly drawn one. Most people don't have to pay federal estate or inheritance taxes, which do not begin until the value of the estate reaches $60,000 ($120,000, if it's a husband or wife who inherits). But you are almost certainly worth more than you think.

A man earning $12,000 a year, who owns a modest house and has kept up his GI insurance and has some work-related insurance as a fringe benefit of his job, will probably leave an estate valued at $40,000.

In the past, lawyers have always worked on client's wills for very low prices. In farming country, the will was virtually thrown in as part of the general service a lawyer did for a regular client. (Experience indicated that clients remained most loyal to the lawyers who helped them with their will.) Today nearly all lawyers do charge, though most charge very little.

For a "simple will, no assets" — whatever that means — a 1970 ABA survey of minimum fee schedules showed one county bar association (Cameron County, Pennsylvania) suggesting as low as $5, and relatively few as high as $50.

For wills *with* assets, the state bar of Texas has had a sliding scale minimum fee schedule that has been published by the ABA. It provides for a fee of one-half of one percent on the first $15,000 in the estate, one-fourth of one percent on the next $10,000, one-fifth of one percent on the next $75,000, one-tenth of one percent on the next $400,000, and one-twentieth of one percent on all money over and above half a million. A man who projected his assets to $40,000 would pay $130 for a will; a man disposing of assets worth half a million dollars would pay $650.

Where the money really comes from

Fees are low partly because lawyers expect to make their money not on the writing of the will but on functioning as an "executor." An executor is a person who makes sure that the terms of the document are carried out, and gets well paid for it. Quite a lot of abuse of dead men's money occurs in this connection, though the problem is worse in some jurisdictions than in others.

The subject was given an attention-getting airing around 1965 after a mutual-fund salesman named Norman F. Dacey wrote a book called *How to Avoid Probate*. It was a nationwide best seller for more than a year. Lawyers were furious about it, not in the usual self-interested this-will-cost-us-money way, but with honest rage over the distortions and dishonesty and misinformation they felt permeated the book, which dealt with ways of avoiding probate court with its attendant guardians and executors. The Connecticut Bar Association was particularly angry, because nearly all the illustrations were drawn from Connecticut, especially from Fairfield County, Connecticut, which was Dacey's stamping ground. But after a meeting of lawyers called to do something, somehow, several of the leaders of the state bar association withdrew from the committee. One of them said, off the record, "It isn't Dacey who's smeared us, it's those guys in Fairfield County. They're just greedy. They've been getting away with murder."

Judges can assign fees to executors according to the work they have actually done or according to the size of the estate they are supervising. For this reason, and especially if you will be leaving an estate of some size, your will should specify payment to executors only on an hourly basis.

If a larger estate does indeed require more time from the lawyer-executor handling it, he should be paid more; if it doesn't require more time, he should not be given the right to take more out of the pot simply because the pot is bigger.

Much of the criticism of fees in estate and probate work is unfair to the individuals involved. What has happened, in brief, is this:

Over the years, the compensation structure of the legal profession developed in the US, lawyers did lots of work for clients for very little money. They prepared tax returns, got the kids out on bail, drew contracts of various sorts, wrote the wills, negotiated with the bank, smoothed over domestic storms in a style closer to that of the father confessor than to that of the courtroom lawyer.

For each of these services, the lawyer charged much less than his time — or the job — was worth. Then, after the client died, the lawyer got his reward in the form of probate and/or executor's fees.

In today's highly mobile America this makes no sense at all: a faraway lawyer becomes the beneficiary of the compensation structure when he charges conventional fees that once were figured to cover a lifetime of service, not just the job of the executor.

Now the lawyers must move to a compensation structure which assumes the laborer is worthy of his hire at each step of the job. That's obviously more sensible and fairer over the long run, but it does mean that some fees go up, which is by no means easy to sell to clients. When lawyers begin to charge for writing wills strictly according to the time involved, the fees

in most cases will be higher than the minimums suggested by the Texas bar.

Lawyers' advice and ability to nail down formal documents are important at the beginning as well as at the end of life, for children
who become part of a family through choice
rather than through natural process.

Adoption is a legal process of considerable com-
plexity for reasons precisely the opposite of those that
make wills and estates so complicated. The dead man
can't change his mind, and the law wants to make
sure nobody changes it for him. But the natural mother
of the child put up for adoption *can* change her mind
(and so can the father) — and this creates a terribly
painful and difficult problem every time it occurs.

When adoption was informal

Once upon a time there was a good deal of informal
adoption. Death in childbirth was common in the
nineteenth century, and so was a fairly heartless aban-
donment, when the parents went west and left the
children behind. If a man left his wife and children and
she remarried, it was commonplace for the new husband to take the children into his own family, changing names without telling any court or registrar
about it.

Today this sort of thing is unwise, because almost

Hoary cliche about wills has mourning survivors astonished
to hear themselves cut off from expected bequests in favor of
unexpected heirs. Supposedly done out of malice,
things of this sort can also happen when wills are drawn up ineptly.

everybody carries around a trail of property of some sort, and getting the succession to this property straight requires formal proof of status. If your brother and his wife are killed in an airplane crash and you add their son and daughter to your own family, you would be wise to undertake the nuisance and expense of a formal adoption. Otherwise the courts will assign quite a number of chiefs for your poor little Indians.

If you are adopting a child through a social service agency, you will be at the mercy of the social workers, who always have lots of applicants for the child they are offering you and will tell you the terms on which you take the baby, leaving little (probably no) room for negotiation. Adoptions from a private party, however, which often involve some compensation to the mother giving up her child, should be negotiated by an experienced person. In any event, a court will have to approve the final agreement, and a lawyer will be needed to draw it up.

Though there are a few counties where lawyers' fees for handling an adoption are under $100, something between $150 and $200 is the most common price. In some counties of New York and New Jersey, the suggested minimum in 1970 was $350; and by now you may be asked as much as $500 in those states, because the local laws make adoption quite complicated. These fees are for technical work in looking over adoption papers prepared by a social agency, checking out the facts, and doing the necessary in the courtroom. If extended negotiations are required, the lawyer may add the cost of his time in the negotiations.

Biologically related to adoption law is the paternity suit, by which an unwed mother tries to prove that a given man is the father of her child and should be compelled to pay for its upbringing. As befits the accidental nature of the situation, these cases are usually carried on a contingent fee, though the lawyer may demand a retainer before beginning work. Economically related to the paternity case is the non-

Another instance of don't-do-it-yourself, get-a-lawyer:
a paternity suit. The services of a lawyer, for either side, can
sometimes be retained on a contingent-fee basis.

support case, where a mother alleges that the admitted father of the child — usually a husband from whom she is separated — has failed to pay what he should pay for his child's welfare.

When welfare supplies a lawyer

Sometimes a city welfare department, saddled with expenses that could be carried by a father who has reneged, will force a mother to bring such suits by threatening to withhold welfare checks if she doesn't. In such cases, the welfare department, which will take any back payments the court can squeeze out of the defendant, should itself provide the lawyer, and probably will.

Bankruptcy would not seem to most people to belong in a chapter on such personal matters as wills and adoptions, but it is functionally, in fact, a similar sort of problem. Here again, the state is asked to do an extraordinary service for an individual, and the nature of the service is such that formal requirements must be precisely met.

For most people, a personal bankruptcy is a private and emotional matter, where a good lawyer will give significant advice as well as taking care of the legalistic end of the proceedings.

There are two kinds of personal bankruptcy:

1) a straight bankruptcy in which the debtor's assets are divided up among his creditors and he is discharged from any need to pay whatever those assets have failed to cover;

2) a "Chapter XIII" wage earners' bankruptcy in which a court voids all existing payment schedules and sets up a new plan by which a debtor can pay his creditors out of his salary on a schedule which he can manage.

Because it involves an interference with the rights of the parties under existing contracts — an activity otherwise frowned upon by the US Constitution — bankruptcy is legally very tricky. It is one of those American oddities in which the law and the procedure are federal, but the federal courts and "referees in bankruptcy" are controlled in what they can do by the laws of the state in which the court is situated. Nearly every state has its own category of assets which need not be sold to satisfy creditors in a bankruptcy proceeding. Most allow a bankrupt to keep his house, clothing and certain household goods; in farming states it is not uncommon to have a horse and plow and a number of pigs preserved from the fate of a forced sale.

For specialists only: bankruptcy

Nearly every lawyer writes wills, handles an occasional divorce and can bring a personal-injury suit; but bankruptcy law is for specialists. The lawyer referral service can supply one. There is no point discussing a possible bankruptcy with a lawyer unless you are prepared to level with him, detailing all assets and all liabilities, and why you can't pay your bills. He will know whether your situation entitles you to bankruptcy (if you've been bankrupt before, within the last six years, you can't do it again;) whether it makes sense for you to sacrifice your assets, which may be greater than you realize, to be rid of your debts; whether the future disadvantages of bankruptcy will be greater than today's benefits (there are a number of licensed occupations for which bankrupts are not eligible and many personnel questionnaires ask about bankruptcy.

Though bankruptcies can be prepared on an assembly-line basis — and are handled that way, by armies of clerks, in some California law firms, for example that specialize in this field — the work to be done before the technicalities are performed makes the service oddly expensive. It's hard to get a bankruptcy done for under $250, and that's cash on the barrelhead, because the lawyer doesn't expect to stand in line with the creditors. But if you really can't pay your bills, and can see no prospect of ever paying them, it's cheap at the price.

Bankruptcy, of course, implies borrowing: if you don't have debts, you can't be bankrupt. Most people who wind up in bankruptcy court are there not because they have foolishly overextended their credit but because they've had some piece of bad luck — illness, accident, unemployment. Some, however, are in trouble simply because they borrowed so much that the monthly payments got beyond their ability to pay. And others may be considering bankruptcy as the only way to escape creditors who are hounding them.

When you buy anything on the installment plan, the contract you sign with the lender gives him certain claims on your current assets and future earnings.

If the product turns out to be defective, you still owe the lender — always a different corporate entity from the merchant who sold you the goods — and you must keep paying. If you don't, the lender may foreclose the mortgage if it's real estate, repossess the TV set or automobile if it's consumer goods, and if you've signed a bad installment contract he may cart away things you own as well as the item for which you have failed to pay.

If more money is outstanding, the lender may "garnishee" your salary, requiring your employer to deduct a certain amount of money for him before you are paid. This gives you a bad name with the boss, among other problems. A notice that a salary is being garnisheed is probably the most common single force pushing people into bankruptcy.

Whenever you get a notice that a suit has been brought against you, it's only common sense to take it to a lawyer; and that applies to these credit matters, too. Sometimes, unfortunately, you don't find out until after your creditor has won a judgment against you, because the marshals who were supposed to "serve" you with a notice of suit failed to do so (though they reported to the court that they had).

Nevertheless, a lawyer can almost always put a brief stop to further proceedings with a telephone call, and he can often keep you from being victimized by the tough cookies of the collection agencies.

These credit questions are rarely clear-cut. In most states, the law leans toward the lender, and not entirely without reason — after all, you as a purchaser on the installment plan have the use of the money you

When the bills, the writs, the bill collectors, the subpoenas get to be too much, that's when bankruptcy may be the only way out. For this you should have not merely a lawyer, but a lawyer who specializes in this very tricky field.

were loaned and the car you bought with it, while the lender has nothing but your promise to pay and the legal system that holds you to the promise. Because you signed a piece of paper and owe the money, you have to produce a clear case that you have been dishonestly treated before the law switches to your side. Developing such a case takes time and money, and this is not a contingent fee situation — you have to pay it out yourself, win or lose. Unscrupulous merchants and lenders count on that to discourage you.

We shall discuss in the last chapter some of the new programs to make it easier for you to explore the rights you have and the enforcement processes available to you in what are often penny-ante situations. Even in the absence of these plans, however, you can usually get more than ten dollars' worth of advice out of the ten dollars you will be charged for half an hour with a lawyer on the panel of a bar association's referral service.

CHAPTER IX

Dealing with Governments and Government Agencies

Roughly $125 billion — one-tenth of the Gross National Product (the total annual value of all goods and services produced in the US in a year — is now dispensed by various governmental units in social services for the welfare of private individuals. Government provides inexpensive housing; subsidy to rural electrification co-operatives; free or nearly free medical care; cash for Social Security and welfare; college scholarships and loan guarantees for students; low-interest disaster loans after storms, floods and earthquakes; school lunches; assistance to small businesses; and a very great deal more. For at least a fifth of the population, government benefits are among the most important supports of their lives.

Uncle Sam is a Big Spender. He
makes money available for all kinds
of purposes through all manner of governmental units. As explained below, each
unit is a law unto itself.

Each government program is literally a law
unto itself. In many of them there is no "right"
that can be enforced in court by someone who
considers himself entitled to the assistance
provided by the Act.

A denial of benefits by the Veterans Administration, for example, can be appealed within the VA to a final board of appeals, but that's the end: the law specifically prohibits the courts from reviewing the action of the administrative appeals board, and the courts have never accepted a case seeking such an appeal.

What the courts have done to supervise the activities of many agencies is to require that the agencies give petitioners a "fair hearing" which must follow certain legally directed formal procedures. In plain language, that means lawyers can be useful.

When non-lawyers can do better

People other than lawyers can be useful, too — sometimes more useful. If you have been denied a payment under Medicare, for example, a doctor friend who knows some of the people in the local Medicare office may be able to get the decision reversed more quickly than any lawyer could do it. If you have been cut off from welfare, a social worker in a neighborhood volunteer agency who knows some of the decision-makers in the welfare department may get you restored much quicker than a lawyer could.

Often, a great service a lawyer can perform is to threaten to waste everybody's time with endless hearings. In agencies that are not geared up to process hearings through a separate semi-judicial process — i.e., the people who do the daily work are also the people who would have to be involved in the administrative appeal — this sort of threat can be very effective.

In school systems, for example, the appeal of an order expelling a child from school — or assigning him to a special school for "problem children" — will have to be heard by some assistant superintendent who would otherwise be doing other things, and the principal of the school will have to be in attendance.

Under these circumstances, a lawyer needs no special talent to get an expulsion changed to a five-day suspension; all he has to do is write a threatening letter. And even if you can't afford to pay a lawyer to follow through at a hearing, you can easily afford the price of a threatening letter. Poor people can get the full service free through a poverty-program law office.

Other agencies, however, have semi-judicial court systems built into their tables of organization: at these agencies hearing examiners process claims and senior examiners process appeals, with little involvement by the top bureaucrats. The examiners don't mind being kept busy.

Keeping the fees unattractive

In general, agencies try to control lawyer involvement in their work by establishing fee schedules that make the cases rather unattractive. The rules of the Rural Electrification Administration, for example, restrict lawyers' fees to $17.75 an hour, which guarantees that only the youngest and least busy county-seat lawyer is likely to put any considerable amount of time into working on cases dealing with the REA.

The Social Security Administration permits lawyers who are working on a contingent fee to represent petitioners who feel themselves cheated of Social Security benefits, but it restricts the enforceable fee to a payment per hour on a rate set by the Administration, *or* 25% of any lump-sum past-due award (nothing on future benefits), whichever is lower.

You *may* pay more if you wish, but any contract to do so cannot be enforced.

If you take the SSA to court, the maximum fee a

lawyer can get is 25% of the past-due benefits. And after a court case you *can't* pay more than that, whether you wish to or not because a lawyer who takes more than the court-awarded fee in a Social Security case commits a crime.

One of the most common sources of dispute between government and citizen is the government's power to seize your house or place of business by the "right of eminent domain," paying you only a "fair market value" that may or may not in fact be fair, and that does not in any event cover the costs you will incur if you have to move away from where you are now.

You cannot stop the government from taking your land, but it is almost always unwise to accept a first offer. (That offer will rarely tempt you, anyway.) If you cannot negotiate a price with the government authority involved, you are entitled to a "condemnation hearing" at which a judge or a jury or a real estate board (depending on the state and the law) will determine a "fair market value." And if that decision still seems unfair to you, you may be able to take an appeal to the courts.

You almost certainly want a lawyer to represent you in these matters, but the best man in
town may not be the lawyer you want. Here
political clout counts for more than ability.

A city councilman, state legislator or congressman
— all eager to do favors for constituents — may be
your most effective spokesman. Many lawyer-legis-
lators will cooperate with you or your lawyer. (Contact with a legislator may also be the best way to
handle disputes with other government agencies —
and in these disputes his help may cost you nothing
but a stamp.)

If there are a number of people with situations
similar to yours, you may even get a legislator to
intervene in his law-making capacity. The introduc-
tion of a bill in the legislature by an assemblyman
got a group of homeowners in Queens, New York,
enough leverage to force a new design for a big high
school that was going to destroy their homes; and
those few who had to lose their property anyway
were paid about three times as much as the city had
initially offered.

Any lawyer can handle these cases, however, and
you may be able to make an interesting kind of contingent fee arrangement that guarantees you against

loss: the lawyer's fee is a proportion (at least a quarter, and often half) of the *increase* in the final price as against the initial offer.

The leverage a lawyer gives you derives from the fact that the government agency is in a hurry. By the time the final funding authorization comes through for the project, the architect has completed his work and the agency wants to get things rolling — especially in our inflationary era. The threat that the lawyer will find some plausible grounds for court action — and repeated appeals — is a very serious one for the agency, which must avoid delays at almost any cost.

When a governmental agency
announces it is taking over your
domestic property to put a road
through, you need a lawyer. He
can dicker with the agency on the compensation this exercise of the right of
eminent domain will bring you.
Usually the first offer made to you
is much, much, much lower than
the one you can fight for and get.

In the building of New York's Lincoln Center, for example, the late Joseph Kennedy twice took the board of that city- and state-sponsored arts center all the way up to the state's highest court to protest what he considered an inadequate price for a warehouse he owned on the site. In the end, the plans for construction had to be changed, and the building designed for that site — which had to be built first — was moved to another part of the Center so work could begin.

Especially if you have a small business on the land the government wants, you should not feel the slightest hesitation about urging your lawyer to try every trick in the book. If you sold your business to someone, he would pay for the "goodwill" — the intangible asset that every going business has in its name and established commercial relationships. But the state, taking the property under eminent domain, will pay nothing for the value of the business it may have destroyed. If the fear of delay and the cost of delay extort from the government more than can be justified by the value of the land and fixtures, that's no more than fair.

Except in situations that involve property, however, it isn't easy to get help from the courts when you are quarreling with a governmental agency.

Part of the essence of administrative process is that administrators have discretion, and discretion means — within limits — a right to be wrong. When the Civil Aeronautics Board awards a route to one airline rather than to another, the loser cannot raise in court the factual questions it raised when the matter was still pending before the agency. So long as there is evidence that the hearing examiners and the commissioners considered the issues, the courts (at least in theory) will not interfere with their findings.

The only hope of winning a reversal is a demonstration either that the agency did not consider pertinent data, which is a hard one to win (among the chores of the opinion-writing staff of a government agency is going over the arguments raised by the losing side and listing them to prove that they were in fact considered), or that the agency in making its decision was following an internal policy different from that intended by the lawmakers who wrote the law.

This sort of policy-oriented lawsuit can only rarely be brought by individuals on their own behalf, because it's an expensive case to prepare. (Corporations can do it, of course, and do, but usually for rather different purposes: they are not trying to get the government to do something they want but to keep the government from making them do something they don't want.)

In recent years, however, with the help of Ralph Nader's young lawyers and the "neighborhood law offices"set up under the poverty program, individuals and groups have been able to start what are really "class actions" to change the policies of a bureaucracy with the power to award or refuse favors.

Neighborhood law offices have been effective in many fields. Years ago states enforced a "residency requirement" on welfare applicants: if you hadn't been in the state for, say, six months, you could starve to death and the welfare department wouldn't put

When eminent domain gets ready to roll over your business, be it ever so humble, compensation should include payment for goodwill as an asset in addition to the value of the property and the business as such.

up a penny to feed you. Tenants in public housing projects had almost no rights in their relations with the housing authority, which treated them as lease-less "month-to-month" tenants subject to eviction for almost any reason. The interstate highway system cut swathes of concrete and fence through neighborhoods. Children charged with crime could be sent to what was in effect a jail without the right to have lawyers cross-examine their accusers.

All this, and much else, has been changed by means of lawsuits brought in the courts by legal aid societies and university-based "law centers" as well as neighborhood law offices. The results do not necessarily always produce benefits to the community. One key public housing case, for example, involved an attempt to expel a middle-aged couple whose son was an

ex-con and a dope peddler, believed to practice his trade when he came visiting the folks. The courts ruled that the housing authority could not evict anyone just because the son of the family was a menace to the health and welfare of the neighbors. Obviously, this decision was no benefit to the other families living in this apartment house.

This is not to say the decision was "wrong," just to note that making policy is more complicated than deciding cases.

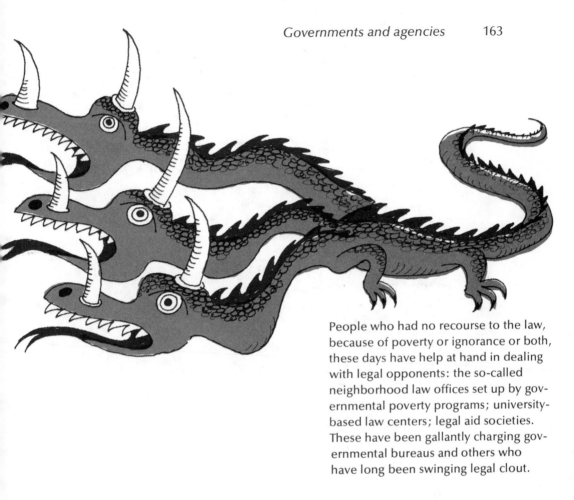

People who had no recourse to the law, because of poverty or ignorance or both, these days have help at hand in dealing with legal opponents: the so-called neighborhood law offices set up by governmental poverty programs; university-based law centers; legal aid societies. These have been gallantly charging governmental bureaus and others who have long been swinging legal clout.

Still, it has been a matter of no small importance that in America in the last decade poor people have been able to proceed in the courts against the policies of government bureaus. The question of the opportunities available to middle-income people in this context dovetails with the subject of the last chapter.

The government agency most people are most in touch with on a regular basis is the Internal Revenue Service. It is probably best to regard this contact as the source of incentives given you by the government rather than as a conduit for the simple extraction of cash from your pocket.

A subsidy is no less a subsidy when it arrives in the form of a tax deduction than it is when it arrives as a stiff green check.

The government encourages you to own a house rather than to rent an apartment, by allowing you to deduct from your income for tax purposes the real estate taxes you pay as a homeowner and the interest you pay on your mortgage. The government encourages you to speculate in oil drilling, to invest in growth stocks rather than mature companies, to keep your savings in municipal rather than corporate bonds — all this through patterns of differential taxation, commonly known as "loopholes."

When accountants do it better

Until fairly recently, 50 years ago or so, lawyers prepared people's tax returns as part of their general legal service, and it would not be true to say that they generously gave up this work to others. The others, mostly accountants, took it away, with the lawyers complaining bitterly, and even suing the accounting firms for practicing law without a license. Nevertheless, most of the work associated with the tax returns of ordinary individuals does not require the expertise of a lawyer. (Corporations and very rich individuals present different problems.) Accountants can do it cheaper, and probably better.

The quality of the tax advice the average person will get from the average accountant is probably higher than the quality of the tax advice he will get from the average lawyer. The accountant lives closer to the problem, and devotes more time to it.

The great contribution of the lawyers is the maintenance of the distinction between tax avoidance (which is perfectly legal) and tax evasion (which is perfectly illegal). If you are rich enough to profit by exploration of the many gray areas within which these categories are distinguished, you will need the help of a lawyer, and you will doubtless be receiving it already. Otherwise, relations with the Internal Revenue Service are probably the clearest example of the value of the maxim about paying the two dollars. When IRS agents examine your return and you, the presence of a lawyer is likely to be a negative factor, convincing the agent that you must *really* have something to hide.

Proceedings before the tax court are complicated and expensive in terms of lawyers' time — and the average aggrieved citizen is not likely to get much more out of such proceedings than he can get by writing a letter protesting a tax assessment and requesting a refund.

"Pay the $2" most often is the
wisest answer when you have a
disagreement with the Internal Revenue
Service. In the overwhelm-
ing majority of cases, the IRS
people are fair and just in applying
the income tax laws. If you believe
an error has been made in auditing your return,
write a letter — coolheaded
— to make your point, but pay the $2.

Perhaps because the American tax system rests on voluntary reporting and public cooperation, people who work for IRS *are* conscious of the fact that they are public servants, and not, in the end, masters. They can be wrong; very infrequently, they can be crooks; but mostly they will apply the law that's in your favor as well as the law that's against you.

The sort of courteous attention to your argument that you need a lawyer to gain from most other government agencies is given more or less automatically by the IRS. It's only when you've done something so wrong-headed that you stand in danger of criminal prosecution, or when the sums of money involved are really large that it makes sense to hire a lawyer to help you with your taxes or tax planning.

CHAPTER X

The Future of
Lawyers
in the US

Central to the beliefs and practices of the American legal profession on the subject of ethics is the notion that lawyers have personal and specially protected relationships with their clients. No lawyer can be made to reveal what a client has told him: all such communications are "privileged." Though the American Bar Association's Canons of Ethics do in fact permit a lawyer to represent conflicting interests (providing both sides know he is doing it), most lawyers would say that they owe an undivided and absolute loyalty to each client.

The next step is to say that working for one man while another man is paying you creates a divided loyalty. Thus the organized bar has always insisted that there must be no intermediary between lawyer

The relationship of lawyer and client is one of
complete confidentiality. No see, no hear, no speak is the
motto of the lawyer, who cannot be made to reveal
anything his client has told or shown him.

and client, that the client must pay his bills himself.
Exceptions to the rule could be made only in cases
of indigence, where insistence that a client pay the
lawyer himself would mean there was no lawyer.
Automobile clubs that provided lawyers for members charged with reckless driving were ordered to
stop doing so in several court cases, and even a group
of nonprofit hospitals was forbidden to run an office
which provided collection services for all of them.

In 1963, the Supreme Court made a hole in the dike, ruling that a state could not prohibit a service provided by the NAACP, supplying lawyers to all who wished to sue on grounds of civil rights.

The next year, the Court blew down the wall, in the *Brotherhood of Railway Trainmen* case, which specifically approved a union program that established a panel of lawyers who agreed to charge union members less than the prevailing rates (25% rather than 33 1/3%) on personal-injury cases. In return for

A case involving a railway workers' union, in 1964,
was a landmark on the long road to group legal programs.
The court approved a program allowing a panel of
lawyers to charge union members lower rates on personal-
injury cases than the prevailing rates.

this agreement, the union recommended these lawyers to injured members.

Three years later, the Court went even further, ap-
proving an arrangement by which the United Mine
Workers hired a salaried lawyer to handle workmen's
compensation cases for members at no cost whatever
to them.

Though the opinions of the Supreme Court were
clear and strong, the lawyers could not believe what
happened to them. In 1964, a distinguished committee of California lawyers produced a report recommending that the bar of that state (a quasi-official
body to which all lawyers must belong) should support rather than forbid programs of group legal services, whereby labor unions and other existing groups
could buy legal services for their members. The board
of governors of the California bar rejected the report.

All over the country, bar associations fought delay-
ing actions to preserve the old one-to-one relationship between lawyer and client, though some labor
unions began to find ways to help their members
secure legal services at lower prices.

In 1971, in one of Justice Hugo Black's last
opinions, the Supreme Court put its foot down
on bar association obstructionism. "Collective
activity undertaken to obtain meaningful access
to the courts," Justice Black wrote, "is a funda-
mental right within the protection of the First
Amendment."

In the summer of 1972 the American Bar Association yielded gracefully: its House of Delegates passed a resolution calling on all state and local bar associations to help organize "plans for providing prepaid legal services."

By the summer of 1973, there were two thousand union-sponsored prepaid legal services programs in the US and the number was still growing.

And during the course of that summer, Congress passed and the President signed a bill amending the National Labor Relations Act to permit unions to include group legal service plans among the fringe benefits that management could be asked to pay for union contracts.

The new congressional bill would make programs to provide such services a legitimate union demand in collective bargaining, enabling union members to buy lawyers' services with what looks like their employers' money. The United Mine Workers and the United Postal Workers began to make such demands even before Congress acted.

Union-sponsored plans fall into three categories. The least common — and the least likely to grow — is the arrangement by which a lawyer hired by the union handles members' legal problems.

Where such plans are established, they will probably be restricted very narrowly in the sort of problem they accept: workmen's compensation and unemployment insurance are the only likely areas. A union plan in Columbus, Ohio, however, offers the help of salaried lawyers in all sorts of legal matters, even criminal cases.

The most frequently encountered union plan offers a "closed panel" of lawyers. It gives members a credit toward lawyers' fees and court costs for a wide range of legal services. (Personal injury is excluded, as are business deals.)

But these credits can be used only to buy the services of a relatively small number of lawyers who would be members of the panel. This arrangement enables the union to control both the quality and the costs of the services provided to the membership — quality because the union investigates lawyers before accepting them on the panel, costs because the panel lawyers are required to subscribe to a maximum fee schedule.

The "open panel": a third system

What the bar associations want is a third system, an "open panel" which would allow the credits

from the prepaid plan to be spent in any law office in
town. A model of this system has been in operation
since early 1971, for the benefit of the members of

The time may come when a member of a group
legal insurance organization may simply present a kind of
"voucher" to gain access to prepaid legal service.

a nearly all-black laborers' union in Shreveport, Louisiana. The plan buys:
• up to $100 worth of consultation-and-advice time in visits to a lawyer's office;
• an additional $250 worth of service per year for letter-writing, conferences and negotiations (with the first $10 to be paid by the client);
• plus up to $475, including court costs and witness fees, for courtroom and administrative hearing work (the first $25 to be paid by the client);
• plus "major legal expense" insurance of up to 80% of the first $1,000. Lawyers charge customary rates, as doctors do in Medicare.

Legal coverage for 2¢ an hour

In the first two years of operations, the Shreveport plan brought an average fee per matter of $142 to the members of the local bar. The cost to the members of the union was 2¢ an hour, or about $40 a year for a man employed full time, which in the rather low-cost community of Shreveport was enough to put the service on roughly a break-even basis. Excluded from the coverage were contingent fee cases, tax returns, class actions, and "shopping" — i.e., seeking the advice of more than one lawyer on the same matter.

Another possible model for the future grows out of the Berkeley Co-op in California, which has formed an organization called Consumers' Group Legal Services, Inc. For $25 a year, co-op members get an education program in how to avoid and/or handle your own legal problems, two free consultations with a staff lawyer, and access to a panel who have agreed to a maximum fee schedule below the prevailing rates in Berkeley.

The American Bar Association Special Committee on Prepaid Legal Services recommended in May of 1973 a model plan not unlike the open panel pioneered in Shreveport, which could be organized by any group. The optimum size of the group, the Committee thought, would be about one thousand families. The "basic benefits" would be a "legal checkup" worth about $35 in lawyers' time, plus $105 worth of advice and consultation, a service that "may include payment for preparation of a simple document."

The checkup, supposedly a parallel operation to a medical checkup, would see to it that the plan member's legal documents were shipshape, and his legal exposure minimized. Additional benefits offered under this plan would cover as much as $3,725 worth of lawyers' time, with a $25 deductible clause; and there would be a further "major legal expense" coverage of 80% on the next $1,000. The exclusions would be roughly those of the Shreveport plan, but the costs would be considerably higher — the ABA committee estimates that $180 a year "would provide a reasonable range of benefits."

Another possibility is a legal insurance policy similar to medical insurance policies.

The New Jersey Bar Association has been in negotiations for several years with Blue Cross, hoping to establish a system that could use the hospital insurance company's administration apparatus. And in California in early 1973, Fireman's Fund Insurance started a pilot program for a legal services insurance plan offering a choice of four policies with different

Some advocates of prepaid, group legal insurance see it as a legal counterpart to a prepaid medical insurance policy. They even foresee a time when a new policyholder would begin by having a "legal checkup" to find out what his immediate situation is and what his future needs will be.

degrees of maximum protection. The premiums were estimated from $41 for the least extensive to $100 for the most elaborate.

The market research study preceding the development of Fireman's Fund policies had indicated that about a quarter of all American households are interested in purchasing some form of legal insurance.

Insurance Company of North America (INA) has also expressed an interest in this business, and has been developing a pilot program with the Philadelphia Bar Association.

So far, none of the prepaid legal services plans seems to have provoked the burst of nasty little lawsuits that some experts feared would be the result of making recourse to the courts free (or nearly free) to what is, after all, a fairly quarrelsome population in this country.

Experience with medical fringe benefits in union contracts and medical insurance programs still makes some authorities fear, however, that similar systems in legal services will lead to gross inflation in lawyers' fees and unnecessary elaboration of the business.

Nevertheless, the outlook late in 1973 seemed to be that group legal services might be coming down the pike at about the time that no-fault insurance greatly diminishes personal-injury law business.

Another factor: the number of students in the law schools has nearly doubled in the last decade. So the new "delivery systems" for legal services would be coming into widespread use at a time when there will be a surplus of lawyers, and that should hold fees down.

Exclusion of "class actions" from the early versions of prepaid legal services plans argues that the middle class will still not have easy access to the sort of law-suit that the poverty-program law offices have been pressing on behalf of poor clients. But, of course, middle-class families are much less dependent on government agencies than the poor are, and have less need for lawsuits of that sort. They also have much stronger influence on what lawmakers do in Congress and in the state legislatures.

Eliminating the mystery

Eventually, much of the mystery that now surrounds legal services will disappear. People who need the services of a lawyer will not have to hunt about to find one, or to wonder what they should pay.

By the mid 1980s, most families will probably participate in one or another form of legal services insurance plan, just as most families today benefit by some form of health insurance. And the existence of the panels that serve the group plans will take some of the element of luck out of the choice of a lawyer when you need one.

People who are concerned about the danger that at some point they will have to employ a lawyer for an expensive piece of work — and more people should be concerned — can now do something about it. You can't buy legal insurance yet, and there are still only a handful of union locals or other groups that offer prepaid services. But the sooner you raise the issue in your own union or business or professional association, the sooner you will have the chance to protect yourself against future costs for legal services.

Legal insurance will not make contact with lawyers much more pleasurable, any more than medical insurance makes it a delight to visit the doctor's office; but like medical insurance it may become an indispensable way to cut your risks in what will always be an unsafe world.

GLOSSARY

The definitions of terms most often encountered in discussions of law and lawyers are made available here — but not for the purpose of helping you make legal decisions on your own behalf. As explained in the body of this book, the purpose is to make your thinking of lawyers and the law realistic and informed. The definitions which begin below will help you understand more of the legal matters you read about in the press or watch on television — because these make up much of the basic and precise vocabulary of American (and English) law.

A

abandon
To surrender one's right or claim of ownership to property or special privilege, i.e., the right to cross someone's property.

abate
To put an end to.

abdicate
Formally to relinquish power over, or responsibility for, a privilege, a right, etc.

abet
To encourage or assist in the carrying out of an illegal act.

abeyance
A condition in which ownership of property or other right is held to be undetermined.

abide by
To accept the consequences of.

ability
Having the legal power to perform an action.

abjure
To renounce under oath a right, claim, title, etc.

abnegate
To renounce or give up one's claims or privileges.

abortive
Fruitless.

abrogate
To abolish with authority a law, or annul, repeal.

abscond
Leaving quickly and secretly to avoid arrest.

absolve
To release one, as from an oath, a legal obligation.

abstain
To refrain from action by choice.

abstract
A summary of the most important points in a document.

abstract of judgment
A short summary of the essentials of a recorded judgment.

abstract of title
A short history of a title to real property.

abut
To be next to.

accede
To agree.

accessory
One who aids a lawbreaker in the commission of a crime but is not present at the time of the crime. He or she can be an accessory before or after a crime.

accomplice
One who aids a lawbreaker either as an equal or as an accessory.

action, to bring an
The right of an individual to exercise his access to legal process by bringing suit against another.

adduce
To present as proof in an argument.

ademption
The loss of a specific bequest in a will when the bequest is nullified because the property is no longer part of the estate.

ad hoc
Referring to a specific case or instance.

ad infinitum
With no limit as to time.

adjourn
Suspend a hearing or other legal operation until a later — perhaps unspecified — time.

adjudge
To determine guilt or innocence, fault or blamelessness, etc. by judicial procedure.

adjure
To command one to testify under oath.

administrator
A person appointed by a court to dispose of an estate of one who dies without leaving a valid will.

admiralty
Law pertaining to international waters — "international" sometimes being interpreted extremely broadly.

affiant
One who makes an affidavit.

affidavit
A written declaration made under oath before a notary public or other person authorized to certify depositions, signatures, etc.

affirm
To make a formal declaration but not under oath.

affray
A public brawl.

aggrieved party
To consider oneself treated unjustly by a court decision or that of any other legal authority.

agreement
A properly executed, legally binding document.

aleatory
An agreement dependent upon the outcome of an event which cannot be foretold.

alibi
A defense whereby a defendant seeks to prove he was elsewhere than the location of the crime when that crime was committed.

alienate
To transfer ownership of property or other possessions.

alienist
A physician who has been accepted by a court as an expert on the mental competence of witnesses.

alimony
Allowance made under court order for support of an ex-spouse in separation, divorce or annulment proceedings.

allegation
An assertion that is not proved or supported by evidence.

allude
To make an indirect reference to.

altercation
A noisy quarrel.

amalgamate
To consolidate, combine.

ameliorate
To improve.

amenable
To be legally responsible.

amend
To alter formally.

amicus curiae
Person invited or permitted to advise a court on an action in which he is not a party.

ancillary
Subordinate, secondary.

anguish
Extreme physical or mental pain.

animosity
Open enmity, active hatred.

annotate
To furnish with explanatory notes.

annul
To declare void.

anomalous
Abnormal.

appeal
To apply for transfer of a lawsuit to a higher court in order to overturn the verdict of a lower court.

appease
To satisfy a claim, as by paying a fine or penalty.

appellate
A judicial unit with the power to hear appeals from decisions made by lower courts.

appendage
Something added, as to the main body of a document.

appraisement
An evaluation of property by an appraiser appointed by a court.

arbiter
Someone chosen or appointed to decide a matter according to the rules or law: as distinguished from an arbitrator.

arbitrary
A ruling set by a court rather than by established law.

arbitrator
One appointed to settle a dispute, not necessarily according to the rules of law.

archives
Public records. Also the place where public records are kept.

arraign
To call someone before a court to answer to an indictment, or charge.

arrest
to seize and hold a person by authority of the law.

arrogate
Unlawfully to take or assume some control or right, or assign same to others.

arson
Malicious burning of the property of another, or one's own for illegal reasons.

aspersion
Criticism or censure: sometimes slander.

assail
To attack violently with physical force or with words.

assault
An attempt to injure someone physically, or a threat to do so.

assent
Agreement.

assess
To set the amount of a fine or a tax, or to estimate value of property for taxation.

assign
To transfer property rights, or interest, or other valuable considerations.

assurance
A pledge or promise to perform an agreed-upon act.

at bar
An issue being considered by a judge.

attenuate
To reduce in force or effect or criminality.

attest
To certify under oath or by signature.

attorney at law
One who is qualified by training and certification to represent a party in a court of law, to prepare, manage and argue his case.

audit
To examine and verify, as a balance sheet, statement of income, etc.

authenticate
To certify as genuine.

aver
To make a statement formally asserted to be a fact.

axiom
An established rule, principle or law.

B

bail
Security posted for the release of an arrested person guaranteeing his appearance for trial.

bailiff
Courtroom attendant.

bankrupt
One who is legally insolvent.

battery
Unlawful use of physical force against a person. Usually coupled with "assault."

bearer
One who holds a negotiable instrument — check, bond, etc., made out to "bearer."

bench warrant
A document authorizing search of premises, etc., issued by a judge or court.

bequeath
To give property, possessions, etc. by will.

blackmail
To attempt extortion by threat of exposure of alleged or real criminal activities or other embarrassing factors.

blatant
Deliberately conspicuous, as in "blatantly" offensive.

bogus
Fake.

bona fide
In good faith.

bond
A certificate or other evidence of obligation.

breach
A violation of a legal obligation, agreement or promise.

brief
A document containing all the facts relative to a specific case, filed by an attorney before arguing the case in court.

burglary
Breaking (as through a closed door or window) in order to enter a building for unlawful purpose.

C

calendar
List of lawsuits pending in a court.

calumny
A false statement maliciously made in the hope of injuring someone.

canon
A body of rules and principles governing the conduct of members of a profession.

capitulate
To surrender, or give up, in a dispute under specified conditions.

carte blanche
Authorization to act without preset conditions.

causa mortis
The cause of death.

cause
A legal case or lawsuit.

caveat emptor
Let the buyer beware.

censure
A severe statement of condemnation for violation of ethics, as in a professional association.

certiorari
A writ to call up the records and findings of a lower court for review by a higher one.

change of venue
Removal of a lawsuit for trial from the original county or district to another in order to obtain a fairer hearing.

charge
An accusation against an alleged wrongdoer. Also, a judge's instructions to a jury before it begins its deliberations after hearing the claims of the opposing sides.

chattel
Tangible but movable property: e.g., a television set, a chair, a cow. In ancient times, also, a slave.

chicanery
A move, or series of moves, to induce a belief in something fraudulent.

183

cite
To order or summon one to a legal hearing; or to refer to a legal authority or precedent in support of a proposition.

class action
A suit instituted for a group of persons with a common complaint against an alleged offender.

clemency
Leniency in punishment granted a convicted offender.

client
One who retains an attorney to represent him.

codicil
A supplement to a will.

coerce
To compel, to take an unwilling action by physical pressure or threat of harm.

cognizance
The examination of a case by a court.

collusion
Secret agreement between two or more parties for fraudulent purposes.

common law
Laws based on accepted usage, not on formally established statutes.

common property
Property owned jointly by a husband and wife, or by members of a group.

commutation
A reduction of the original penalty, or sentence, that was to be served by a person found guilty in a suit.

compensatory damages
Damages assigned by a court to compensate for losses by a plaintiff.

complaint
Plaintiff's presentation in a civil action setting forth a claim for damages sustained.

condemn
To pronounce judgment against.

confiscate
To appropriate property by the exercise of legal authority.

conservator
A legally appointed guardian or custodian.

contempt
Openly expressed disrespect and/or willful disobedience of the authority of a court of law or legislative body.

contest
To dispute a charge or accusation.

contingent
Conditional. E.g., an award for damages may be made contingent on presentation of proof of costs.

contract
A formal, binding agreement between two or more parties.

convene
To assemble in a traditionally constituted manner for a public purpose.

convey
To transfer title.

corporation
A group of persons, e.g., a business company, authorized to act as a single legal entity.

counselor
Lawyer, attorney-at-law, person authorized to represent clients in a court of law.

covenant
A formal sealed agreement or contract, usually without any termination date.

culpable
Deserving censure.

D

damages
Money paid or ordered to be paid as legal compensation for injury or loss.

decedent
A person who has died.

deed
An instrument transferring ownership of real property.

de facto
In reality, in actuality.

defamation
Slandering or otherwise causing injury to the public reputation of a person.

default
Failure to appear, pay, or otherwise act as legally ordered.

defendant
A person against whom a legal action is brought.

defraud
To cheat.

defray
To pay, costs and expenses, for example.

delinquent
Past due.

demurrer
The entry of a formal objection to being required to make a pleading of guilty or not guilty in a legal action.

deposition
Written testimony obtained through direct and cross-examination.

deputy
One authorized to act for another.

detainer
Unlawful withholding of the property of another.

devise
To bequeath real property by will.

disbar
To revoke an attorney's right to practice.

dissent
To disagree with the majority opinion.

divest
To take away from.

divorce
Dissolution of a marriage by law.

docket
Calendar of cases awaiting a court's proceedings, or a brief summary of the results of a court's proceedings.

doctrine
A rule or principle established by law.

document
A written or printed instrument designed to furnish decisive information for a legal hearing.

dogma
A principle or belief generally considered to be authoritative truth, particularly in religion but also in law.

domain
Ownership of property, with the right of disposal.

domicile
Legal residence.

dower
That part of or interest in a deceased man's real estate allotted by law to his widow for her use during her lifetime.

E

easement
A right given a person to allow a limited use of another's real property: e.g., to drive or walk across a prescribed area of it.

edict
A decree with the force of law, being issued by a sovereign source.

egress
Exit, and/or the right to use it.

elicit
To draw out information from a private or hidden source.

embargo
To prohibit the movement of goods from one point to another.

embellish
To add undocumented, imaginative or fictitious details to a narrative or document.

embezzle
To take someone else's property for one's own use in violation of a trust.

eminent domain
The right of a government to appropriate private property for public use, as for a highway.

enact
Establish by law.

encroach
Gradually (and usually stealthily) to intrude upon another's property or right.

encumbrance
A lien or claim upon property by someone other than the owner of record.

enjoin
To use legal means to pro-

hibit someone from taking a specified action.

equity
The value of an owner's, or owner's interest in a property.

equivocal
A statement or action that is capable of more than one interpretation.

escheat
A political unit's power to take over, or confiscate, property for which no one else can make a valid claim.

escrow
Putting into the custody of a third party valuable considerations to be held until certain conditions are fulfilled by the two parties to the agreement — for example, to buy and sell property.

estate
An individual's assets.

estop
To prohibit an action inconsistent with an individual's or group's previous position, particularly if anyone has taken action on the basis of the statement of the previous position.

et al
And others.

ethics
Moral or other principles governing conduct of certain groups, such as doctors of medicine, elected public servants, etc.

et ux
And wife.

evict
To force out from the premises a tenant, house-dweller or other occupant by legal process.

evidence
Documented or verbal statements and the material objects admitted as testimony in a court of law.

evoke
Call forth or cite, as, e.g., a precedent.

executor
One named in a will to carry out its provisions.

exemplify
To make a certified copy of

a document from public records.

ex officio
An act or decision performed by virtue of the office held by the person acting or deciding.

exonerate
To free from a charge.

ex parte
From one side only.

expire
Cease to be effective.

extort
To obtain money or information by coercion or intimidation.

extradite
To surrender an alleged criminal to another (usually international) authority for trial.

F

facsimile
An exact copy.

fee simple
An unrestricted title to real property.

feigned
Pretended, false, phony.

felony
A crime considered more serious than a misdemeanor; examples: murder, rape, burglary.

fictitious
False.

fiduciary
A trustee.

foreclose
To deprive a mortgagee of the right to redeem a mortgage.

forfeit
A penalty.

fraud
A deliberate deception practiced for unlawful gain.

freehold
A term covering a number of types of ownership of real property.

G

garnishment
Proceeding requiring one who holds money or property for another not to dis-

pose of or direct the disposition of the money or property without court order.

germane
Pertinent.

good will
The value of an established relationship of a business enterprise with its customers, recognized as an intangible asset of the enterprise.

grand jury
A jury empowered to evaluate, usually in secret, accusations against a person charged with a crime and to determine whether the evidence presented warrants a public trial.

grand larceny
Theft of property exceeding a specified amount; a greater crime than simple larceny.

grant deed
Written instrument by which real property is transferred.

gravamen
The core of a legal complaint.

grievance
An actual or supposed circumstance regarded as a proper cause for complaint.

guarantee
To assume responsibility; the responsibility so assumed.

guardian
A person who is legally responsible for the care of another because of age, physical or mental incapacitation.

guilt
Legal responsibility for a crime committed against established law.

H

habeas corpus
A writ issued to bring an imprisoned person before a court or judge for the purpose of determining whether the person held should be released temporarily from restraint.

harass
To disturb someone repeatedly in a manner calculated to cause acute discomfort, either mental or physical.

hearing
Preliminary examination of
an accused person.

hearsay
Evidence based on reports
of others rather than on the
witness' own knowledge,
usually not admissible in a
court.

hiatus
A gap, or break, in continuity,
as of ownership, for example, or control.

hoax
An act designed to deceive.

holographic will
A will made out in the hand-
writing of the maker.

homestead
Property designated by a
homeowner as his home and
protected by law from a
forced sale to meet debts,
as in bankruptcy.

hung jury
A jury which fails to agree
upon a verdict.

hypothecate
To pledge property as security to a creditor, but without
making actual transfer or
transferring possession.

illicit
Prohibited by law.

immaterial
Of no legal importance.

immune
Exempt.

impartial
Unprejudiced.

impeach
To charge with, and try for,
wrongdoing in public office.

impede
To block.

impinge
To encroach upon, to tres-
pass against.

impound
To hold in custody.

impugn
To attack as false.

impunity
Being exempt from punish-
ment.

inalienable
Not to be transferred or
given away.

incapacitate
To make legally ineligible.

inculpate
To incriminate, charge,
accuse.

indefeasible
Not capable of being
annulled.

indemnify
To insure.

indemnity
Insurance against or com-
pensation for damage, loss
or injury.

indenture
A deed or contract executed
between two or more parties.

indict
To make formal accusation
of wrongdoing by the findings of a grand jury.

inebriate
Habitual drunkard.

inequity
Injustice.

infamous
Notorious, known for bad
reputation.

infant
One under legal age of
majority.

infer
To conclude from evidence.

infraction
Violation.

infringe
To violate.

inhibit
Restrain.

innuendo
A hint or implication, usually derogatory.

in propria persona
Acting on one's own behalf.

inquest
Judicial inquiry.

intangible
Something of substance but
incapable of being precisely
defined.

interim
An interval of time between
one period and another.

intermediary
One who acts as go-between
between persons.

interpolate
To insert new material into
a document, particularly to
change its aim or conclusion.

interrogate
To examine a witness by
formal questioning, usually
under oath.

intervene
To come between two
parties in a dispute.

intestate
Having died without making
a legal will.

inure
Accrue to the benefit of
someone, particularly by
usage.

invalid
Without force.

invoke
To cite a precedent or legal
finding.

ipso facto
By the fact itself, as in
"condemned ipso facto."

jaywalk
To walk across a street
illegally.

judge
One qualified and desig-
nated to make binding
decisions in legal disputes.

judgment
A formal decision of a court.

judiciary
A system of courts of justice.

jurisdiction
Having the right to exercise
power.

jurist
Lawyer, judge or other person knowledgeable in law.

jury
A group of persons sworn to
hear and give a verdict upon
a case presented in a court.

justice
Lawfulness.

juvenile
Legally still a child, pre-adult.

L

larceny
Theft.

lawsuit
Case brought before a court.

legacy
Money or property bequeathed to someone by a will.

legitimate
Lawful.

liable
Legally obligated.

libel
Any written, printed or pictorial statement that damages a person by defamation of character.

lien
The right to take and hold or sell property of a debtor for payment of a debt.

liquidate
To pay off or settle a debt or claim; to wind up the affairs of; to convert assets into cash.

lis pendens
A pending suit.

litigant
One engaged in a lawsuit.

litigate
To engage in legal proceedings.

M

magistrate
A civil officer with power to administer and enforce law at a basic level.

majority
Age at which one attains legal rights of an adult.

malfeasance
Misconduct by a public official.

malpractice
Most often refers to improper, negligent or harmful treatment of a patient by a physician but it can also cover improper or unethical conduct by a member of other professions.

mandate
Order issued by a superior court to a lower court.

manslaughter
Murder committed without premeditation.

maritime
Of or pertaining to the sea.

mechanic's lien
A claim for payment for services rendered, placed against a house or other construction, which can thereafter not be sold until the lien is satisfied.

mediate
To settle differences by acting as an intermediary between two or more conflicting parties.

misdemeanor
A legal offense rated lower than a felony.

mortgage
Temporary and conditional pledge of property as security against a debt.

municipal
Pertaining to a city or its government.

N

negate
Nullify, to render ineffective.

negligence
Not taking reasonable care or action in carrying out a function.

nolo contendere
Plea by a defendant that he is unwilling to contest a charge but does not plead guilty.

nonfeasance
Failure to perform an act that is an official duty or legal requirement.

non sequitur
Literally, something that does not follow. I.e., an inference or conclusion drawn that is not based on established evidence.

notary public
A public official authorized by law to certify documents, take affidavits and administer oaths.

notice
A formal announcement.

nuisance, creating a
Use of property or behavior that interferes with the legal rights of others by causing damage, annoyance or inconvenience.

nullify
Make void, render ineffective.

O

object
To take exception to.

obligate
To bind.

obstruct
To block an act by another.

offense
A transgression of law.

onus
A responsibility or burden, usually disagreeable.

optimum
The best condition for a particular situation.

option
A portion of an agreement left open to final decision by either party.

ordinance
A statute or regulation enacted by a governmental unit smaller than a state.

P

panel
A list of persons summoned to be interrogated for possible assignment to jury duty.

paraphrase
A restatement of a legal text in another form, often to clarify meaning.

parole
Release of a prisoner for good behavior in jail before his term expires on condition of continued good behavior.

party
A person or group involved in a legal proceeding.

penalize
To subject to a penalty for an infringement of a law.

penalty
A punishment established by law for a crime or offense.

pending
A term used for a legal action which has not yet been decided.

peremptory
A legal ruling made under conditions allowing no debate.

perjury
Knowingly giving false testimony under oath.

perpetrate
To be guilty of.

per se
By itself.

persecute
To harass, make uncomfortable.

persona non grata
A person who is not acceptable or welcome.

petit jury
A trial jury, empowered to decide on guilt or innocence, as distinguished from a grand jury, empowered to hear evidence and indict for trial.

petition
A formal written application requesting a court action for a specific judicial decision.

plaintiff
The party who institutes a legal suit.

plea
A statement offered in support of a plaintiff's case.

posthumous
Occurring after the death of the person concerned.

precedent
A judicial decision that may become a standard to be cited in subsequent similar cases.

precept
A principle.

preclude
To take action to prevent something from occurring.

preempt
To take possession of something in order to prevent anyone else acquiring it.

prejudicial
To take an action or make a decision detrimental to any party.

premeditate
To plan a deed, usually illegal, in advance.

pretext
An excuse.

prima facie evidence
Evidence that would establish a legally accepted fact if uncontested.

principle
Accepted as a basic truth.

probate
The legal process by which the validity of the provisions of a will is established and carried out.

proof
The evidence that determines the verdict or judgment in a case.

prorate
To divide proportionately.

prosecute
To enforce a legal decision by legal action.

pro tem
Temporarily.

proviso
A clause calling for a conditional application of a provision in a document.

pseudo
Fake.

pseudonym
Fictitious name.

punitive
Involving punishment.

Q

quitclaim
Releasing a title, right or claim to another without a warranty.

R

receiver
A person appointed to take over property pending the outcome of litigation concerning it.

reconcile
To settle or resolve a conflict between two or more parties.

reconveyance
To transfer ownership of property back to the original owner.

record
An account officially prepared as evidence or testimony.

redress
Make amends for damage or harm.

referee
Someone appointed by a court to examine and report on a case.

refute
To prove a statement to be false.

rejoinder
A second pleading by or for a defendant in answer to a plaintiff's reply.

relevant
Related to the matter at hand.

render
To hand down, as a judgment.

repeal
To annul a law, etc., officially.

reply
To answer a defendant's plea.

repossess
To take back ownership of property previously transferred.

reprimand
Formally to express disapproval.

res ipsa loquitur
The thing speaks for itself, i.e., is self-evident.

revoke
To make invalid an order or judgment previously handed down.

S

search warrant
Legal authorization for a search of premises.

sentence
To assign a penalty to a person found guilty.

session
The period during which a court or legislative body sits for the transaction of its business.

set aside
Dismiss or discard.

settle
To transfer property by legal action or to terminate legal proceedings by consent of the parties concerned.

sheriff
A county law-enforcement officer.

sine qua non
An essential element or condition.

slander
Oral statements injurious to the reputation or business of a person.

solvent
Having sufficient assets to meet all financial obligations.

status quo
The existing condition.

statute
A law enacted by a legislative body.

statute of limitations
A statute prescribing the period of time after which no suit may be brought for punishment of a crime or payment for damages, etc.

stipend
Fixed compensation.

stipulation
A term or condition in an agreement.

stringent
Severe.

subpoena
A legal document requiring appearance in court or before a legislative body to testify.

subpoena duces tecum
A legal document requiring production of books, documents or other evidence in court.

sue
To institute legal proceedings against someone.

suit
Lawsuit.

summation
A concluding statement by a plaintiff or defendant summarizing principal points of evidence previously presented.

summons
A judicial order directing a defendant to report to court.

surety
One who gives security for the performance of an obligation of another.

T

tangible
Visible, appraisable.

tantamount
Equal in effect or value.

technicality
A trivial distinction.

tender
An offer of money or service in payment of an obligation.

testament
Last will.

testate
Having made a valid will.

testimony
Oral statements made by a witness under oath.

tort
An injury or wrong committed on the person or against the property of another.

trademark
A distinguishing symbol, for a product usually registered.

transcript
An official copy of a document.

trustee
One who controls property of another, as in accordance with a will.

U

189

ultimatum
A final statement of terms in an argument.

unanimous
Characterized by complete agreement.

V

valid
Legally sound.

verdict
A legal decision.

voluntary
Performed in the absence of obligation.

W

waiver
Intentional relinquishment of a right.

warranty
A promise that goods or property are as they or it have or has been represented.

will
A formal legal document setting forth the manner in which a person wishes his property to be disposed of at his death.

witness
One who has sufficient knowledge to testify in court to a fact or an occurrence.

Workmen's Compensation Act
A statute which provides for fixed awards to a workman or his dependents in the event of an accident to him on the job.

writ
An order of a court directing the person to whom it is addressed to do or refrain from doing a specified act.